By the Ionian Sea

Lost and Found Series

Old Provence by Theodore Andrea Cook
Two Years in the French West Indies by Lafcadio Hearn
The Pilgrimage to Santiago by Edwin Mullins
A Romantic in Spain by Théophile Gautier
The Silent Traveller in London by Chiang Yee
The Silent Traveller in Oxford by Chiang Yee
Coming Down the Seine by Robert Gibbings
Journey to Mauritius by Jacques-Henri Bernardin de Saint-Pierre

*Classic Travel
Writing*

By the Ionian Sea
Notes of a Ramble in Southern Italy

George Gissing

Introduction and Notes
by Pierre Coustillas

Interlink Books

An imprint of Interlink Publishing Group, Inc.
Northampton, Massachusetts

This edition first published in 2004 by

INTERLINK BOOKS
An imprint of Interlink Publishing Group, Inc.
46 Crosby Street, Northampton, Massachusetts 01060

First published in 1901
Introduction © Pierre Coustillas, 2004

Library of Congress Cataloging-in-Publication Data
Gissing, George, 1857-1903.
By the Ionian Sea : notes of a ramble in Southern Italy / by George Gissing.
p. cm. — (Lost and found series)
ISBN 1-56656-494-8 (Paperback)
1. Italy, Southern—Description and travel. 2. Gissing, George, 1857-1903—Travel—Italy, Southern. I. Title. II. Series.
DG821.G5 2003
914.5'70484—dc21

2003013526

Cover Design: Baseline Arts
Cover Image: John Heseltine Archive

Printed and bound in Canada by Webcom

Contents

Introduction by Pierre Coustillas   vi

The Manuscript   xxv

Acknowledgments   xxvii

CHAPTERS

1	From Naples	1
2	Paola	7
3	The Grave of Alaric	14
4	Taranto	22
5	Dulce Galæsi Flumen	29
6	The Table of the Paladins	36
7	Cotrone	44
8	Faces By the Way	52
9	My Friend the Doctor	60
10	Children of the Soil	68
11	The Mount of Refuge	75
12	Catanzaro	82
13	The Breezy Height	93
14	Squillace	100
15	Miseria	107
16	Cassiodorus	112
17	The Grotta	119
18	Reggio	124

Notes   133

Further Reading   152

Introduction

By Pierre Coustillas

George Gissing, known to modern readers and historians of English literature as a late Victorian novelist bent on denouncing the social evils he observed around him, was a man of two worlds: the world in which poverty and other handicaps compelled him to live, and the classical world in which, from childhood onwards, his imagination sought refuge. When, at the end of his 25-year career, he felt the need to reminisce and offered the reading public a volume of meditations on his artistic experiences, he lent his semi-autobiographical character, Henry Ryecroft, a confession which was at once illuminating and potentially misleading: "I had in me the making of a scholar. With leisure and tranquillity of mind, I should have amassed learning. Within the walls of a college, I should have lived so happily, so harmlessly, my imagination ever busy with the old world."

His 22 novels and a hundred-odd short stories of modern life have easily eclipsed Gissing's single travel narrative, not to speak of his fascinating but unfinished novel of sixth-century Rome. As a result, despite all the praise lavished upon *By the Ionian Sea* in England, the United States and Italy since its original publication, Gissing has remained essentially the author of *The Nether World*, *New Grub Street*, and *The Odd Women*. Only Samuel Vogt Gapp, in his 1936 study *George Gissing, Classicist*, gave his undivided attention to the importance of Gissing's statement on the eve of his journey to the deep Italian South: "The names of Greece and Italy draw me as no others, they make me young again [...] The world of the Greeks and Romans is my land of romance." Unfortunately, because his material was limited to the printed, as opposed to the manuscript, material available at the time, Gapp could not enquire very deeply into his subject and size up correctly what is now called Gissing's Mediterranean passion. Free access to manuscripts, unpublished notes and correspondence remained an unfulfilled ambition, and successors in such a field do not spring into existence at one's bidding.

Gissing's mental life, whether in full consciousness or (at least twice) in delirium, was haunted by the sources of western civilization and its early flowering in Greece and Italy, and only a justified concern for the marketability of his work held him back from writing other books with pronounced historical leanings than this volume about Magna Græcia and his novel *Veranilda*, which it partly overlaps. He is reported to have made allusions to the prospective use in fiction of ancient times as late as 1903. The young man who in 1876 wrote a lyrical piece entitled "Italia" and confessed that:

Like exile's, pining for his home,
My heart leapt at the name of Rome

and the experienced novelist in whose mind a historical tale set in Rome in the days of Cicero was shaping itself were the *other* Gissing. He still largely awaits the recognition of enlightened critics.

✻ ✻ ✻

Nothing in Gissing's geographical and social origins predestined him to write *By the Ionian Sea*. Born in Wakefield in 1857, in what used to be the West Riding of Yorkshire, he became acquainted in infancy with the heavy industrial pollution to which he was often to refer in his correspondence. Local mill-owners cared more for profit than for the purity of air or water. The writer's father, Thomas Waller Gissing, an essentially self-taught pharmaceutical chemist, was aware of this, and in his political action on the Liberal side, he did his best, with scant success, to remedy it. He himself the son and grandson of humble shoemakers who had never left rural Suffolk, fought for forms of progress which harmonized with his intellectual and artistic aspirations. Botany and poetry were his passions and he published three booklets of verse as well as two volumes on English ferns and on the flora of Wakefield. Wordsworth and Tennyson were among his preferred authors.

Realizing that George, his eldest son, was an extremely gifted and precocious child, he encouraged him in his eager quest for culture, which was all-comprehensive and included notably literature, history, art and languages. Young Gissing was a prize-winner, and the juvenilia he has left us in the domains of prose and poetry is clear testimony to his great intellectual and artistic potentialities. Save for his uncommon shyness, all went well in his school and home life until 1870, when his father, who had overworked himself and paid scarce attention to his declining health in the last few years, died of respiratory disease.

Together with his two brothers, George was sent to a Cheshire boarding school whose principal, nominally a Quaker, conformed selectively to the teachings and practices of his sect. Gissing's hatred of militarism can be traced back to those hours of drill to which he was unwisely submitted once a week. From 1872 to 1876, after he had come first for the Manchester district in the Oxford local examinations and won a scholarship that enabled him to continue his studies at Owens College, now the University of Manchester, he distinguished himself in Latin, Greek and English. He was a poor, hard-working, brilliant student very much like Godwin Peak in his outstanding novel *Born in Exile*. At the time he read and reread the historian Edward Gibbon, whose presence is felt more than once in the background of *By the Ionian Sea*, as he did John Forster's Life of Dickens, when he needed some intellectual stimulant. At the end of those four years during which he matriculated and passed his first BA, his scholarly future looked brighter than ever and the prospect of a university career was definitely within reach.

But an amatory temptation to which, as a lonely student living in poor lodgings, he unfortunately yielded, ruined his hopes of making his way in adult life as predicted by his teachers and fellow students alike. He attempted to redeem a girl of the streets he was in love with,

Marianne Helen Harrison (Nell), who was one year his junior and, when he became short of money for her, rifled the pockets of his fellows in the college cloakroom. In late May 1876 he was caught red-handed (officially the marked money found in his own pockets amounted to five shillings and twopence), arrested, sentenced to one month's imprisonment with hard labour and, of course, expelled from College. Nell being in his eyes a victim of a cruel society, he had acted rashly and was to suffer to the end of his life the consequences of his self-destructive approach to a never-to-be-solved social problem, although in the opinion of those who followed his career with full knowledge of his youthful folly, he lived down the scandal. The scrupulous honesty he henceforth evinced, together with a deep-rooted tendency to self-mortification, were to inform his conduct at critical moments of his emotional life and professional career.

Thanks to funds collected by the college authorities, who were seriously disturbed by the affair and felt some remorse for not having dealt more humanely with a poor scholarship boy, thanks also to the generosity of a few friends of the Gissing family, his mother exiled him to America. There, it was hoped, he would make a fresh start in life. But he did not. Neither in Boston, where he only succeeded in publishing one article on a painting exhibition, nor in Waltham, despite a short teaching experiment, did he put down roots. The assistance of a few culturally influential Americans, with whom Owens College professors had put him in touch, proved of no avail. Instability began to rule his life. He made a new—heroic—attempt to find some profitable occupation, leaving Waltham abruptly for Chicago, where, now aged nineteen, he embarked on a literary career, contributing short tales to the local press. The story of his relationships with the editor of the *Chicago Tribune* and a few men in similar positions has been investigated with notable success in the past twenty years or so. However, in the autumn of 1877, having written himself out, he had to acknowledge his defeat and, with considerable difficulties, made his way back to England, where his mother gave him a chilly welcome.

Gissing at once settled in London, where Nell joined him in sordid lodgings, the first of a series of homes that were no homes, which he graphically described in *The Private Papers of Henry Ryecroft*, his bestselling book for many years. For about a decade, that is until he at length managed to make a living of sorts by his pen, he did odd jobs, essentially badly-paid private teaching which nonetheless gradually put him in touch with a few upper-class families, whose superior airs sometimes irked him. As he soon realized after his return from America, Nell was not redeemable and her irresponsible behaviour was to him a permanent burden as she became a slave to drink, bent on associating with unruly lower-class women. Nonetheless, unwilling to disregard his commitment of the Manchester days and spurred by an ingrained masochism, he married her in October 1879, although by then he was convinced she was past redeeming. Three years later he parted from her, but continued to send her a weekly allowance to the end, which came in February 1888, when she died in a Lambeth slum, crushed by drink and syphilis.

Although not deliberately autobiographical, Gissing's first published novel, *Workers in the Dawn,* throws abundant light on the world in which he lived in the late 1870s. His material difficulties were pathetic. The book is artistically faulty on account of its profuseness, for which the irrational system of publication of fiction in three volumes encouraged by circulating libraries was more responsible than the author. Yet a few perceptive critics, while acknowledging that the young author still had to curb his powers and learn the expediency of restraint, ventured to predict that this first novel "emphatically offer[ed] a promise of something great." His brief socialistic sympathies already belonged to the past as before long would his acceptance of the Positivist credo, in the wake of which should be seen his collaboration, through Frederic Harrison and Ivan Turgenev, to the progressive St. Petersburg monthly *Vestnik Evropy* in 1881-82. *Workers in the Dawn* inaugurated the phase of his working-class fiction in 1880 and was followed until the end of the decade by four more titles on which his early reputation was largely based, *The Unclassed, Demos: A Story of English Socialism, Thyrza* and *The Nether World,* the darkest and most powerful of the series. It was an arraignment of the deplorable living conditions of the London poor partly inspired by his wife's death. Relative success only came with *Demos,* and it was aided by anonymous publication at a time when riots broke out and social peace briefly seemed to be in danger. The intelligentsia wondered who could be the author of this lively picture of popular life, but of his earnestness and artistic talent no one had any doubt.

His subsequent works were seen in the same light, but no wide popularity loomed ahead. Gissing treasured the good opinion of *The Unclassed* that Meredith and Hardy had expressed, privately rather than publicly. Popular success would have disquieted him. The two incursions he made into provincial middle-class life with *Isabel Clarendon* and *A Life's Morning* were the prelude to the widening of his thematic spectrum which took place concurrently with his two long stays abroad, first in France and Italy from September 1888 to February 1889, then in Greece and Southern Italy during the next winter. From his tender years in Wakefield, where he had begun his apprenticeship of the classics, later reflected in the lively conversations between Waymark and Casti in *The Unclassed*, he had longed to visit the shores of the Mediterranean and to see at close quarters the most significant of those sites that were landmarks in ancient history. Now that, as a result of Nell's death, he could consider himself free in all respects and that the sale of his novels spared him the worst fears attendant on poverty, his major cultural dream could at length come true. His diary and correspondence for those years abound with details about his various intellectual quests, notably for Greek and Roman civilizations, and, to a lesser degree, the artistic flowering of the Renaissance.

The novel he wrote between his two Mediterranean trips, *The Emancipated*, heralds the main theme in E. M. Forster's early works, *Where Angels Fear to Tread* and *A Room with a View*. The liberating power of the Italian way of life greatly benefits, morally and spiritually, the less benighted minds among those English tourists who have ventured as far south as Naples and other beauty spots with romantic names. *The Emancipated* also foreshadows the thematic exploration that his novels of the last decade of the century offered to the élite among the English reading public. Within a few years he dealt with the commercialization of literature resulting from the development of education since Forster's Education Act and published his acknowledged masterpiece, *New Grub Street* (1891), then with the conflict between scientific rationalism and traditional beliefs in *Born in Exile* (1892), whose protagonist Godwin Peak has been compared with such major figures of the European novel as Raskolnikov, Bazarov, Niels Lyhne, Robert Greslou, and much closer to us, Camus' masterly creation, Meursault. In 1893 he went on with what now appears to have been his main contribution to the so-called "woman question", *The Odd Women*, a fictional study of that large number of single females of marriageable age which caught the eye of dozens of novelists of both sexes at the turn of the century and became the raw material for quite a few genuine period pieces. As usual, though studying a subject that, strictly speaking, was hardly a brand new one, Gissing showed his originality. Margaret Walters rightly observed in her introduction to the Virago reissue of the book that "it is the novel's central, life-giving paradox [that] seen as failures and misfits, pushed contemptuously to the margins of life, the 'odd' women hold the key to a better future." After analyzing a mode of mental liberation in *The Emancipated*, he had somewhat unexpectedly shown that hope might, phoenix-like, be resuscitated from the ashes of despair. Professional activity and equality of rights between the sexes were Gissing's solution to the "woman question". He predicted an era of sexual anarchy, but was prepared to trust nature. Whether this was his last word on the controversial topic is at least doubtful. *In the Year of Jubilee*, which came from his pen a year later, showed that some avenues in the land of anarchy could prove to be mere blind alleys and, when a manner of supplement to this vision of couples undermined by an urban life that was just as hectic as unprofitable was commissioned by an enterprising editor, he wrote the ironical *Eve's Ransom*, which depicts the provisionally happy fate of a young woman putting an end to her emotional hesitations by marrying money—a case of self-ransoming by forfeiting one's freedom.

Gissing had now reached the apex of his career. From 1895—the signal was given by the journalist Henry Norman in an article on the memorable meeting of the Omar Khayyám Club on 13 July—he was generally regarded, with Meredith and Hardy, as one of the three best living English novelists. He himself was not sure that a service had been done him. Better than his self-appointed judges, he knew that his professional future might be gravely affected by external elements. True, his work was in demand—since 1893 he had launched into a second career as a short story writer and his annual income had risen measurably—but, as two novellas, *Sleeping Fires* and *The Paying Guest*, published in quick succession, suggested, the danger of over-work lay ahead, and he may already have feared that his health was beginning to decline. Even more importantly, his mental peace had been perturbed for some time, for he had remarried in 1891, and this second marriage, again to an uneducated young woman, Edith Underwood, was proving as disastrous as the first, the situation being made worse by the birth of a child in late 1891, followed by that of another in early 1896.

Nevertheless, the next long novel he wrote, *The Whirlpool* (1897), partly concerned with domestic and educational problems, somehow benefited from his unstable private life. It is by any standards an impressive work whose merits have been attracting considerable attention of late. Even so, with its completion coincided the early signs of lung trouble which, despite several periods of remission, was ultimately to prove fatal. But while he completed *The Whirlpool*, mentally sustained by his hostility to the absorbing political developments of the age, notably the rising manifestations of imperialism, he remained positive. Besides, a new area was thrown open to him just then: he received an offer to contribute a critical study of Dickens' works to be included in the Victorian Era series. Writing this book on a familiar subject would have to be postponed until after he had kept a promise to let his agent have the text of a short novel for serialization, but he did not shudder at this prospect: for one thing, criticism of Dickens would be a welcome change from grinding out fiction, for another his faculties were stimulated rather than hampered by the proximity of deadlines. Unfortunately in early February 1897 a double crisis played havoc with his plans: his wife's violent behaviour drove him away from his Epsom home, and his deteriorating health made it necessary that he should go and recuperate his strength in the mild climate of Devon. From mid-February to the end of May, he reread Dickens, making notes for his critical study, and immersed himself in the works of Cassiodorus and St. Benedict that he planned to turn to account in a sixth-century novel which was slowly taking shape in his mind. Unwittingly perhaps, he was in that historical world which serves as a bridge between *By the Ionian Sea* and *Veranilda*.

A half-hearted attempt at resuming matrimonial life with his shrewish wife having failed during the holiday they took in the Yorkshire Dales once the serial story entitled *The Town Traveller* was completed, Gissing set out to reorganize his life and that of his wife and children. By mid-August his decision was made. He first expressed it clearly though obliquely in a letter of the 18th to a literary correspondent, Herbert Heaton Sturmer, who had first written to him about one of his short stories the year before: "I have been seriously meditating a flight to Italy—especially as I am much occupied with historical studies relating to Magna Græcia. The familiar land beckons me as I lie awake at night among these Yorkshire hills, I hear the song of the Calabrian peasant, & see the colours on mountain and on sea." He admitted that he was beset with difficulties of all sorts, which he explained, but in retrospect, we clearly see that he was carefully planning all the steps to be taken prior to his departure. The next day he told Bertz, his German friend, that he was "just busy with a delightful book,—Lenormant's 'La Grande-Grèce,'" adding that he had only intended to study the pages relating to Cassiodorus, the monk and statesman whose name remains attached to that of the Visigothic king Theodoric and to the Calabrian mountain town of Squillace. A wealth of details about his preparations for his journey, material and otherwise, are supplied by his diary and correspondence. Hardly was he back in his Epsom home, where he had lived since September 1894, when he travelled north again so as to inform his Wakefield relatives of his plans, writing ominously to another friend, Dr. Henry Hick, that life was uncertain.

✳ ✳ ✳

Gissing left London for Milan, finally settling in Siena on 26 September at an address with a picturesque name, 18 Via delle Belle Arti, and in a no less picturesque atmosphere concentrated on the composition of his *Charles Dickens, A Critical Study*, which kept him busy until 5 November. It was hard work, each day bringing him 1,000 words closer to the end, but necessity spurred him on. He nonetheless managed to see much of the singular town every evening after he had done his daily quantum. His landlady, and the other lodgers, who included a genial though quirky young American, Brian Ború Dunne, whose scrappy recollections of him remained inaccessible until recently, offered him welcome company. His next preliminary stages, quite logically, were Rome, which he had not seen for nine years, and Naples, where he stayed with a family to whom we are introduced in the opening chapter of the book. At the British consulate, not unwisely, he had his will executed by the consul, Eustace Neville-Rolfe, author of *Naples in the Nineties*. The vice-consul procured for him information about the boats to Paola and, while walking about the town, he formed some idea of the numberless changes that had occurred while the *sventramento* materialized. Would he ever be able, as he had hoped since he had become acquainted with his works, to read Theocritus in Sicily? His curiosity was at its height as he left Naples by the Florio boat at 12 o'clock on 16 November.

Gissing's route cleverly associated his interest in the ancient Greek settlements with that in one of the enigmas of Gothic life in the early fifth century AD. Since the Naples-Messina boat stopped at Paola, why, he had thought, should he not land there and give himself a chance of forming a personal opinion as to the old topographical problem concerning the grave of Alaric? If no public carriage could take him to Cosenza, a private one could be hired. This is what he did once he was on shore at 8 a.m. on the 17th, leaving Paola in a rickety carriage at 10 a.m. and reaching Cosenza at 4 in the afternoon. He did not tarry near the supposed site of Alaric's burial, and took the train to Taranto two days later at 7.10 a.m. As an opportunity to see the plain of Sybaris was not to be missed, he made a halt there for a few hours, having lunch at the station hotel, impressed by "this great southern plain, so still and dreamy." Then, his mind busy with all that he wished to see in and near Taranto, he stayed five full days in the land of Horace and Virgil and had a pleasant time with the English vice-consul, Wilfrid Thesiger, on his fortieth birthday, the 22nd. It was a happy, profitable stay, as would be that in Catanzaro, even though there vestiges of the past dated back no further than the Middle Ages. Early on the 25th he took the train to Crotone, making a new halt at Metaponto on another plain. The remains of the old Greek temple were the only attraction, but to Gissing

Metaponto was the place where Pythagoras died, a refugee from Crotone. He did not reach his destination until 10 p.m.

There is no doubt that he had not planned to stay in that insalubrious town for ten days, but he had to make a virtue of necessity. Only the combination of luck and the ministrations of a local doctor, whom time has made famous, spared him an early grave in what had once been—ironically—one of the healthiest and most famous cities of Magna Græcia. At Catanzaro, where he travelled in the afternoon of 6 December, he stayed on till the 10th in the morning and enjoyed his stay, which the local British vice-consul, Baron Pasquale Cricelli, made as pleasant as possible. In contrast, his next stage—Squillace, where he would gladly have stayed several days—was limited to part of a day after he reached the town in the rain and was received by a crook of an innkeeper. On the same evening he made his way to Reggio by train. There on 11 and 12 December he had two busy, very profitable days, casting a last glance at Etna as he took the train to Naples on the 12th at 7.05 p.m. Twelve hours later he was in Naples again, having seen Paola from a new angle in passing. Save for the sadly impracticable visit to Capo Colonna his dream had materialized—beautifully.

Ideally, sharing to the full all Gissing's experiences would demand of the reader that he or she should follow three methodological routes: that supplied most elaborately by his book, that offered sketchily by the notes in his diary which, besides the informality of the narration, provide information which disappeared in the course of the literary polishing, and that to be found in the traveller's correspondence, rich and varied, which adds much to the other sources owing to the variety of tones conditioned by that of his correspondents, with their respective ages, occupations, personal interests and cultural levels. Treating these sources as a variorum record of Gissing's manifold impressions, moods and delayed responses would produce the richest possible crop on condition that some sidelight were thrown by his notes from Cassiodorus and Lenormant, his essay on the grave of Alaric written at Taranto, and Edith Lister's recollections of Gissing's oral account of his Calabrian journey. It is also appropriate to note that the traveller's writings on the subject, more or less informal or as polished as he could make them after the four-tier editing on the manuscript, the typescript, the proofs of the serial version and those of the book offer a synthesis of successive judgments passed by the author on his own work. There is in his career no similar example, except possibly that of *The Private Papers of Henry Ryecroft*, with its two successive versions, of a text which was composed after some eighteen months' maturation. As well as new, the method would seem to have been deliberate, for nowhere during that period did he record any intention to postpone the actual writing for so long, or, for that matter, any regret at having to do so. It was only after his settling in France with his French translator, Gabrielle Fleury, that he wrote down his reminiscences of his travels from Naples to Reggio, the first nine chapters in the Fleurys' flat at 13, rue de Siam, Paris, from 29 June to 9 July, the last nine at Trient, Switzerland, from 28 July to 9 August 1899.

✳ ✳ ✳

The *Fortnightly Review*, a monthly publication despite its name, published the narrative in five instalments from May to October 1900, but the publication in volume form, an easy matter in principle, was delayed on account of the difficulty in finding a capable illustrator. Calabria was little known outside its frontiers, and Calabrian artists had apparently no contact with English publishers and editors. So Gissing had to help with black and white illustrations—some postcards and photographs purchased in Italy, supplemented by the author's own sketches assuredly met Chapman and Hall's demand—but the desirable colour illustrations eventually had to be supplied by a practically unknown artist from Trieste, Leo de Littrow, who managed to produce full-page illustrations which, though suggestive enough and conveying something of the Calabrian atmosphere, failed to rouse enthusiasm. Once he had proofs in hand, Gissing suspended his judgment, and it may be significant that no publisher since the widely acclaimed first edition came out has been tempted to reproduce the colour illustrations. Collectors have had a weakness for them, but the volume learned early on to dispense with their company.

Although both the narrative course of *By the Ionian Sea* and its philosophical message are perfectly limpid, the book is a complex one. If

Gissing, who had carefully prepared his journey, seems to follow a straight line, the structure of his travelogue is markedly binary. From Naples to Reggio we oscillate between sounds and silence, light and darkness, life and death. Or again between antiquity and modern times, between daily life and noble visions of the past born of imagination, between the pagan world and Christendom. A volume from which the author excluded what he called in another place the impertinent ego, *By the Ionian Sea* is nonetheless a highly personal book, no passage of which could easily be attributed to any of his predecessors or successors who haunted the winding shores of southern Italy, say Ramage or Norman Douglas. But the writer's ego, which, though blurred, is omnipresent in *The Private Papers of Henry Ryecroft*, where Ryecroft is sometimes Gissing unadulterated, sometimes pure fiction, does not intrude here. None of the factual elements of his life, as it is summed up above, appears in the present escapist narration. True, the reader is told lyrically in a paragraph of Chapter I about Gissing's passion for the world of the Greeks and Romans, but on the one hand this exposition is part and parcel of the book and, on the other, it is conducted with notable restraint, in a manner likely to rouse, then increase the reader's expectations. The intellectual enchantment of the writer's youth is fraught with promises which, we know, shall be kept. It is not until Chapter XIII is reached that we come across an understated admission that occasional weariness creeps up on the professional writer, a confession quite in line with the final touch of self-pity "for him who cannot shape his life as he will, and whom circumstance ever menaces with dreary harassment."

It is with another ego that we become acquainted in *By the Ionian Sea*, a largely intellectual ego made up of a myriad elements scattered through his diary, correspondence and private papers, most of which have been published. At one end of his highly sensitive intellectual keyboard loom up the Latin and Greek works he had first studied in his young days and enjoyed rereading as an adult; at the other end the bulky tomes of Cassiodorus' *Variæ* and Lenormant's leisurely account of his peregrinations in Magna Græcia, through which he had gone pen in hand. Indirectly Gissing reveals a major portion of his culture, of which his shallow critics had not suspected the existence, and which, understandably, had never been paraded in the forefront of his fictional works. Here was for the first time a book by him, the twenty-third, written in the first person, which invited readers to look upon his novels of contemporary life from a new angle.

Perceptive critics pointed the way, and the book was brilliantly received. Gissing must have smiled if he read a review like that published in the *Guardian*, the Anglican weekly, which had more than once taken him to task for being too critical of his own country:

> *Mr. Gissing's new book comes as a most delightful surprise to his friends. We knew him as a student of the dreary streets of outer London, and we realised that in him we had a charming writer of stories, an expert novelist, whose latest book was sure of a ready welcome; but there was hardly one of us who was able to appreciate Mr. Gissing that had anticipated a book of travel such as this from his pen.*

Volume and author were praised enthusiastically—the classical scholar, the traveller's humanity, the analyst of social life, the limpid prose, the poetic power of blending the present with the past and re-peopling Greater Greece with the figures of antiquity were all selected for commendation, and the successive editions, whether English, American, Italian or Japanese were greeted with admiration, respect and not infrequently emotion. Doubtless the judgment passed in 1957 by the Italian translator, Margherita Guidacci—"one of the most notable books of the last century on Italy that were written by foreign travellers"—would have gratified a man to whom, next to England, it was Italy's future which mattered most.

Strikingly different though it is from the average travel narrative of its day, *By the Ionian Sea* can profitably be viewed as a link in the long chain of foreign books about the deep Italian South. English and Italian historians and bibliographers of the genre generally remind us of early, little read and very scarce books such as those by Jean Claude Richard Saint-Non and Henry Swinburne, which reflect travelling experiences prior to the epoch-making earthquake of 1783. But the first attempt at a systematic enquiry into the subject was made by the Italian local historian Cesare Mulé in an undated booklet published under the imprint of Gustavo Brenner some forty years ago. Mulé listed and briefly described a selection of English, French and German works written by officers and civilians from the 1790s to the 1960s which enables one to see Gissing's book in context.

Among those original testimonies by adventurous foreign visitors in provinces which were still regarded as dangerous and only partly civilized, one comes across the names of Duret de Tavel, a French officer who equated Calabrians with murderers, of the pamphleteer and Greek scholar Paul-Louis Courier, and of a Swiss military surgeon, Horace Rilliet, all of them memorialists of the Napoleonic period, but also some much better known predecessors of Gissing, like Edward Lear, François Lenormant and Paul Bourget. Strangely enough, however, there is no volume more akin to Gissing's than that of Craufurd Tait Ramage, whose *Nooks and Byways in Italy* was based on a journey made in 1828, but published forty years later. No town or ancient deserted site of classical civilization visited by Gissing had been ignored by Ramage seventy years earlier. Both men are equally eloquent about chance encounters, landscapes and significant ruins. But nowhere does Gissing mention Ramage, whose itinerary, genial turn of mind and learned references to ancient literature and history would have delighted him no less than the scholarly historical excursions of Lenormant, and much more than Bourget's snobbish and mannered *Sensations d'Italie*, in which he cannot have felt the intense cultural involvement so tactfully in evidence in his own book.

German travellers, too, have made a sizeable contribution to representations of Calabria since the Age of Enlightenment, but Gissing, despite his good knowledge of the language and his familiarity with German literature, never mentions any of the travel books discussed in depth by Teodoro Scamardi in his recent study *Viaggiatori tedeschi in Calabria*. There is no reference, for instance, to those of von Riedesel, Friedrich Leopold Stolberg and the future burgomaster of Hamburg Johann Heinrich Bartels, who memorably said in defence of Calabrians that "they are men like us." Bent on rehabilitating the reputation of Calabria, he would certainly have concurred with the transparent suggestions for reform scattered throughout *By the Ionian Sea*.

What John Pemble, in his seminal book *The Mediterranean Passion:*

Victorians and Edwardians in the South, brilliantly demonstrated, namely the steadily growing interest of Englishmen in the warmest parts of Europe, had not reached the vast regions south of Naples. One recalls the severe words of Creuzé de Lesser in his 1806 volume, *Voyage en Italie et en Sicile en 1801-1802*: "Europe ends at Naples; it even does so pretty badly. In Calabria, Sicily and all the rest you are in Africa." By Gissing's time, things had changed, though not considerably. He had noticed the steady evolution described by John Pemble, he was aware that an ever greater number of English people crossed the Channel and enjoyed themselves basking in the Mediterranean sunshine, but he repeatedly observed once he had left Naples that Northerners did not venture south of that city; all the lower part of the Italian boot, compared with the North, remained undeveloped. It is characteristic that the museum custodians he met in Catanzaro and Reggio spoke no other language than their own. The small museum at Metaponto, he was told, had been transferred to Naples; a stranger put in an appearance "once in a hundred years." The English travellers who crossed the Channel and went beyond France did not set foot in that part of the country that was said to lie between Eden and barbarian wastes. Thomas Cook, the apostle of mass tourism, had not realized the potentialities of the South, nor indeed have his successors to this day.

Gissing, for one, fought shy of the average tourist. In *The Emancipated* he had satirized the typical English sightseer that could be met in northern museums or in such glamorous places as Capri, Herculaneum and Pompeii, but he did not have to worry; there were no crowds on the banks of the Galeso or the Esaro. Indeed, one wonders how Baedeker's and Murray's handbooks for southern Italy could have profitable sales. Print runs, were they known, would at least tell part of the tale. Yet travel narratives were readily accepted by the reading public, which, then as now, consisted partly of armchair travellers, to whom the Continent was at once attractive and fraught with dangerous potentialities.

Gissing relished his solitude. Even a congenial, cultured companion in sympathy with his highly specific quest would not have been a welcome presence. Any concession to the likes and dislikes of any man or woman by his side would have spoilt his journey into the past as well as into himself. For an untypical Victorian like Gissing or like Samuel Butler or Norman Douglas, John Pemble rightly observes, the travel book was "a personal testament, describing an inward as well as an outward journey and serving as a vehicle for random fragments of description, opinion, and erudition." Certainly Gissing wrote more about the byways than about the highways of Magna Græcia and he shared his attention between two things that no companion could have fully understood, the permanent, dead world of the Greeks and Romans and their mediæval successors, and the transient world of the present moment, the brief, often pathetic, encounters with, say, a ploughman who seemed to be a reincarnation of some old-time Greek agriculturist or with some latter-day domestic slave like the housemaid at the Concordia in Cotrone. This immersion in an alien yet familiar world was a way of distancing himself from the modern world and its absorbing problems, a way of proving to himself that mental peace, however artificially and temporarily, could be enjoyed if one knew where to look for it. And meanwhile Gissing reveals himself as he had never done in his stories of modern life. He is learned without ever becoming pedantic, open-minded to an unknown degree, his curiosity being whetted by the novelty of the sites he visits. His senses respond to colours, to smells, to the size of exotic vegetables, to the forms and movements of human bodies, to expressions on the faces around him, and more generally to the beauty of landscapes. A major though discreet aspect of the book is its celebration of the hedonistic life, adumbrated in some purple patches of his novels, but never so glowingly expressed as in these pages where pleasure occasionally attains a quintessential form.

Yet Gissing is not blind to the innumerable aspects of life in the South that would depress the idealist. They range from the discomfort he had to bear in some inns reminiscent of public places of entertainment in the Middle Ages to the sorry state in which he found the banks of the Esaro in Cotrone; from the deficiencies of social services to the nefarious existence of a national institution like the *dazio*; from the gross absurdity of papal indulgences to the iniquities of corrupt politicians. Gissing's strictures are refreshingly candid. His determination to be fair to the natives, enhanced by his emotional stance towards the pathos of Italian history, give him an engaging image which goes a long way to account for the warm treatment of the book by Italian critics. There is no record of any disagreement in Italian criticism with Raffaele La Capria, who wrote in 1993 on the occasion of the reissue of Margherita Guidacci's translation: "Rarely have I found in a travel book so much respect and so much delicacy of feeling."

It is true indeed that Gissing is anxious to be just to Italians, especially to Calabrians. He praises their generosity more than once, while mutual kindness is on several occasions in evidence. His visit to the pottery market at Cosenza gives an adequate measure of his liking for Calabrians, which is reiterated in the touching passage about the ploughman and his donkey, "a man so utterly patient" with his beast, "so primævally deliberate". "Pottery for commonest use among Calabrian peasants," we read in Chapter 3, "has a grace of line, a charm of colour, far beyond anything native to our most pretentious china-shops. Here still lingers a trace of the old civilization. There must be great good in a people which has preserved this need of beauty through ages of servitude and suffering." In the Italian sunshine, the sun-worshipper George Gissing was prepared to see the best side of things, and few passages in the book are more nobly inspired than that in which, having recovered from that dreadful fit of fever at Cotrone, he reproaches himself after hearing a street organ for narrowness and ingratitude: "All the faults of the Italian people are whelmed in forgiveness as soon as their music sounds under the Italian sky [...] Legitimately enough one may condemn the rulers of Italy, those who take upon themselves to shape her political life, and recklessly load her with burdens insupportable. But among the simple on Italian soil a wandering stranger has no right to nurse national superiorities." And the same genuine sympathy and humility prevail until the last chapter, when he comments on the sad fate of the poor soldier who fell in a Reggio street, a victim of Bourbon tyranny.

This is Gissing in one mood. There are many others in this volume of kaleidoscopic variety and richness. He can be lyrical as when he expounds his expectations on the eve of sailing for Paola; realistic when watching the fishermen at Taranto; nostalgic in his meditations on the plains at Sybaris or Metaponto; urbane in Don Pasquale's company; humorous at the sight of the two uninspiring officers in the Albergo

Centrale at Catanzaro; or furious when confronted with the dishonest *albergatore* of Squillace, but we share all his humours and attitudes because they all bear the stamp of his indefeasible humanity. A pioneer in his day, Gissing has gone here, as in his unconventional novels and short stories, off the beaten track, he has also, as Manfred Pfister has noted in his anthology *The Fatal Gift of Beauty*, gone against the grain of the prevalent denigration of the contemporary Italian's intellectuality. While admitting that there was no intellectual life south of Naples, he beautifully conveyed the notion—of supreme importance to him—that those Italians of many social conditions he had met during his journey, with the notable exception of the obscurantist mayor of Cotrone, had "an innate respect for things of the mind."

This is one of the many paradoxes in the book and its author. But the most striking paradox is that Gissing, who had an excellent knowledge of Italy, past and present, who had spent months in Naples, Rome, Florence, Venice and Siena, who had conducted immense enquiries into the past of that country whose unification was recent and culturally so incomplete, should have chosen to write of semi-deserted shores. Few better suggestions of *contre-voyage*, far from the hordes of tourists who flock to the major cultural centres, could have been made at the time. Material necessity compelled him, on leaving Reggio, to travel back to his native fog-bound England, significantly stopping at Monte Cassino to pay homage to Saint Benedict, who was to make an appearance at Chapters XXIV to XXVII of *Veranilda*. His journey into the past, as he says in conclusion, an endless, unchartable journey "amid the silence of the ancient world, the present and all its sounds forgotten," could only be imagined nowadays through an immersion in the multitude of volumes of ancient history and literature he is known to have read. But even his more ardent admirers will be content to reread what William Grimes, in a review of *By the Ionian Sea*, called "a record of a golden interlude in a short life filled with hardship and bitter disappointment." Here we have Gissing as close to Paradise as he had ever hoped to be.

THE MANUSCRIPT

The history of the manuscript of *By the Ionian Sea* has been summed up by Arthur Freeman in *George Gissing 1857-1903: Books, Manuscripts and Letters, A Chronological Catalogue of the Pforzheimer Collection* (London: Bernard Quaritch, 1992), p. 27. In the 1920s it was divided into halves. The first was sold by Algernon Gissing, George's brother and literary executor, to Walter T. Spencer, the London bookseller, in 1922; it consisted of the first 18 leaves. The second half, pages 19-35, was sold at Sotheby's six years later (sale of 18-21 June 1928, lot 901). The 35 leaves, written on rectos only, have never been studied closely. One passage on p. 33, neatly crossed out, was published by Jacob Korg in the July 1984 number of the *Gissing Newsletter*. (See note 5 to Chapter 18.) Some accurate idea of the physical aspect of the manuscript may be formed through a careful examination of the facsimile of p. 1 and others laid out fanwise on p.45 of the 70-page Quaritch catalogue. Collation of the manuscript with the first edition shows that the text was extensively revised, but with a very few exceptions the alterations are of a purely stylistic nature; their frequency and number vary considerably. For instance, Chapters 3, 4 and 6 to 8 contain many more changes than chapters 5, 10 and 12 to 18. As a rule they concern a word or a phrase and testify to Gissing's great stylistic care. Thirteen corrections have been made in the text of the present edition: eight of them concern misspellings of Italian words, five misreadings of Gissing's tiny handwriting by the typist that were overlooked by the author.

Two short characteristic passages, untouched on the manuscript, were cancelled either on the typescript which was not preserved, or on the proofs. The first, which shows to what extent Gissing had been incensed by the obscurantist response of the mayor of Cotrone to his innocent request, occurred between the references to hearth money in England and to the hungry plebs of Cotrone: "It would have done me much good if I could have heard the mob proceeding from words to acts; news that the Municipio was in flames would have been to me almost like a return of the blessed sun" (Chapter 9). The second passage was inspired by the rising militarism in late nineteenth-century Italy. It was the conclusion of the paragraph on the latter-day barbarian in civil garb (Chapter 18), which was entirely rewritten: "The wars of old were at least picturesque, and stir imagination in the ringing pages of history; those of our day are irredeemably vulgar, sordid as the wiles of the money-market, where they are plotted and brewed. No poet shall sing the battles of the coming era; their glorious issues shall be yelled by blackguard newsvendors, alternating the name of a triumphant general with that of a winning race-horse." Gissing must have realized, perhaps only at proof stage, that his message would carry as much weight if it was expressed in a quieter tone.

ACKNOWLEDGMENTS

Preparing this edition of *By the Ionian Sea* has been a labour of love. To Gissing, writing down his impressions of southern Italy was not only a self-appointed task, but a cultural delight. Sharing it with him has been a stimulating experience, both human and intellectual. During my four journeys in his footsteps I have been in touch with many Italian southerners whose hospitality and generosity have constantly been in evidence, and it is now a duty as well as a pleasure to record my gratitude to those friends and correspondents who spent time and energy unstintingly to give accurate answers to my many questions. My greatest debt is to Dr. Francesco Badolato, whose knowledge of Calabria is only equalled by his willingness to help. Dr. Renato Santoro has been very helpful concerning matters relating to Catanzaro, as have Signora Teresa Stranieri, Dr. Giacomo Borrino and, at a later stage, Francesca Ammendolia and Maruca Varano Vega. Dr. Domenico Marino has identified his great-grandfather Giulio Marino, whom Gissing mentioned feelingly but did not name; together with his wife Tatiana, he made valuable suggestions concerning some illustrations. Franco Cricelli supplied indispensable details about the vice-consul of Catanzaro. Professor Teresa Liguori threw light on aspects of life in Crotone in Gissing's time, as did Dr. Vincenzo Misiani and Dr. Claudio Sabbione and his wife Carla on events and situations pertaining to the history of Reggio di Calabria. Dr. Mauro Francesco Minervino was a worthy cicerone in Paola and Cosenza; so were Daniele and Tiberio Cristofaro in Squillace, Domenico Napolitano, director of the *Crotonese*, and Dr. Anili in Crotone. Dr. Sergio Dragone, historian of Catanzaro, clarified with authority various topographical details which the mere passage of time seemed to have obliterated.

I should also like to thank Francis Lapka of the Lilly Library for making photocopies of the manuscript of *By the Ionian Sea* available to me; Wulfhard Stahl for sharing with me his topographical knowledge of the places visited by Gissing; and Aurelio Fulciniti for inviting me in his chapter about Gissing to take a fresh look at Catanzaro; and indeed all the friends and correspondents who gave me an opportunity to exchange impressions about the far Italian South.

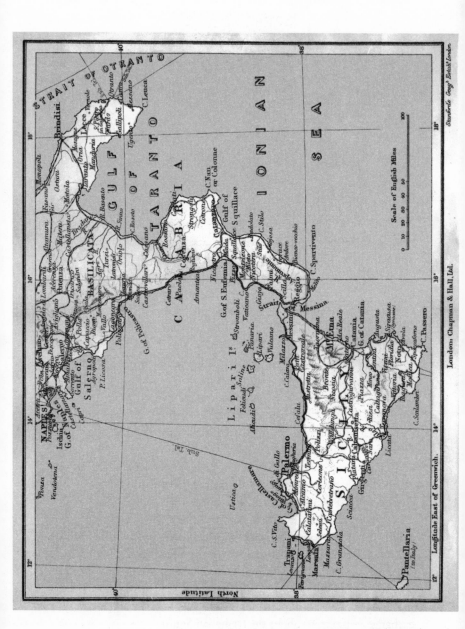

STRAIT OF OTRANTO

GULF OF TARANTO

CALABRIA

IONIAN SEA

BASILICATA

NAPLES

Gulf of Salerno

Lipari Is.

SICILY

Pantellaria
(to Italy)

North Latitude

Longitude East of Greenwich.

Scale of English Miles

Stanford's Geog.l Estab.t London.

London, Chapman & Hall, Ltd.

1
From Naples

THIS is the third day of sirocco, heavy-clouded, sunless. All the colour has gone out of Naples; the streets are dusty and stifling. I long for the mountains and the sea.

To-morrow I shall leave by the Messina boat, which calls at Paola. It is now more than a twelvemonth since I began to think of Paola, and an image of the place has grown in my mind. I picture a little *marina*; a yellowish little town just above; and behind, rising grandly, the long range of mountains which guard the shore of Calabria. Paola has no special interest that I know of, but it is the nearest point on the coast to Cosenza, which has interest in abundance; by landing here I make a modestly adventurous beginning of my ramble in the South. At Paola foreigners are rare; one may count upon new impressions, and the journey over the hills will be delightful.

Were I to lend ear to the people with whom I am staying, here in the Chiatamone[1], I should either abandon my project altogether or set forth with dire misgivings. They are Neapolitans of the better class; that is to say, they have known losses, and talk of their former happiness, when they lived on the Chiaia[2] and had everything handsome about them. The head of the family strikes me as a typical figure; he is an elderly man, with a fine head, a dignified presence, and a coldly courteous demeanour. By preference he speaks French, and his favourite subject is Paris. One observes in him something like disdain for his own country, which in his mind is associated only with falling fortunes and loss of self-respect. The cordial Italian note never sounds in his talk. The *signora* (also a little ashamed of her own language) excites herself about taxation—as well she may—and dwells with doleful vivacity on family troubles. Both are astonished at my eccentricity and hardiness in undertaking a solitary journey through the wild South. Their geographical notions are vague; they have barely heard of Cosenza or of Cotrone, and of Paola not at all; it would as soon occur to them to set out for Morocco as for Calabria. How shall I get along with people whose language is a barbarous dialect? Am I aware that the country is in great part pestilential?—*la febbre!* Has no one informed me that in autumn snows descend, and bury everything for months? It is useless to explain that I only intend to visit places easily accessible, that I shall travel mostly by railway, and that if disagreeable weather sets in I shall quickly return northwards. They look at me dubiously, and ask themselves (I am sure) whether I have not some more tangible motive than a love of classical antiquity. It ends with a compliment to the enterprising spirit of the English race.

I have purchases to make, business to settle, and must go hither and thither about the town. Sirocco, of course, dusks everything to cheerless grey, but under any sky it is dispiriting to note the changes in Naples. *Lo sventramento* (the disembowelling)[3] goes on, and regions are transformed. It is a good thing, I suppose, that the broad Corso Umberto I should cut a way through the old Pendino[4]; but what a contrast between that native picturesqueness and the cosmopolitan vulgarity which has usurped its place! "*Napoli se ne va!*" I pass the Santa Lucia with downcast eyes, my memories of ten years ago striving against

The Strada Santa Lucia in the early twentieth century

the dulness of to-day.[5] The harbour, whence one used to start for Capri, is filled up; the sea has been driven to a hopeless distance beyond a wilderness of dust-heaps. They are going to make a long, straight embankment from the Castel dell' Ovo[6] to the Great Port, and before long the Santa Lucia will be an ordinary street, shut in among huge houses, with no view at all. Ah, the nights that one lingered here, watching the crimson glow upon Vesuvius, tracing the dark line of the Sorrento promontory, or waiting for moonlight to cast its magic upon floating Capri! The odours remain; the stalls of sea-fruit are as yet undisturbed, and the jars of the watersellers; women still comb and bind each other's hair by the wayside, and meals are cooked and eaten *al fresco* as of old. But one can see these things elsewhere, and Santa Lucia was unique. It has become squalid. In the grey light of this sad billowy sky, only its ancient foulness is manifest; there needs the golden sunlight to bring out a suggestion of its ancient charm.

Has Naples grown less noisy, or does it only seem so to me? The men with bullock carts are strangely quiet; their shouts have nothing like the frequency and spirit of former days. In the narrow and thronged Strada di Chiaia I find little tumult; it used to be deafening. Ten years ago a foreigner could not walk here without being assailed by the clamour of *cocchieri*[7]; nay, he was pursued from street to street, until the driver had spent every phrase of importunate invitation; now, one may saunter as one will, with little disturbance. Down on the Piliero[8], whither I have been to take my passage for Paola, I catch but an echo of the jubilant uproar which used to amaze me. Is Naples really so much quieter? If I had time I would go out to Fuorigrotta[9], once, it seemed to me, the noisiest village on earth, and see if there also I observed a change. It would not be surprising if the modernization of the city, together with the state of things throughout Italy, had a subduing effect upon Neapolitan manners. In one respect the streets are assuredly less gay. When I first knew Naples one was never, literally never, out of hearing of a hand-organ; and these organs, which in general had a peculiarly dulcet note, played the brightest of melodies; trivial, vulgar if you will, but none the less melodious, and dear to Naples. Now the sound of street music is rare, and I understand that some police provision long since interfered with the soft-tongued instruments. I miss them; for, in the matter of music, it is with me as with Sir Thomas Browne.[10] For Italy the change is significant enough; in a few more years spontaneous melody will be as rare at Naples or Venice as on the banks of the Thames.

Happily, the musicians errant still strum their mandoline as you dine. The old trattoria in the Toledo[11] is as good as ever, as bright, as comfortable. I have found my old corner in one of the little rooms, and something of the old gusto for *zuppa di vongole*.[12] The homely wine of Posillipo smacks as in days gone by, and is commended to one's lips by a song of the South.

❉ ❉ ❉

Last night the wind changed and the sky began to clear; this morning I awoke in sunshine, and with a feeling of eagerness for my journey. I shall look upon the Ionian Sea, not merely from a train or a steamboat as before, but at long leisure: I shall see the shores where once were Tarentum and Sybaris, Croton and Locri.[13] Every man has his intellectual desire; mine is to escape life as I know it and dream myself into that old world which was the imaginative delight of my boyhood. The names of Greece and Italy draw me as no others; they make me young again, and restore the keen impressions of that time when every new page of Greek or Latin was a new perception of things beautiful. The world of the Greeks and Romans is my land of romance; a quotation in either language thrills me strangely, and there are passages of Greek and Latin verse which I cannot read without a dimming of the eyes, which I cannot repeat aloud because my voice fails me. In Magna Græcia the waters of two fountains mingle and flow together; how exquisite will be the draught!

I drove with my luggage to the Immacolatella[14], and a boatman put me on board the steamer. Luggage, I say advisedly; it is a rather heavy portmanteau, and I know it will be a nuisance. But the length of my wanderings is so uncertain, its conditions are so vaguely anticipated. I must have books if only for rainy days; I must have clothing against a change of season. At one time I thought of taking a mere wallet, and now I am half sorry that I altered my mind. But—

We were not more than an hour after time in starting. Perfect weather. I sang to myself with joy upon the sunny deck as we steamed along the Bay, past Portici, and Torre del Greco, and into the harbour of Torre Annunziata, where we had to take in cargo. I was the only cabin passenger, and solitude suits me. All through the warm and cloudless afternoon I sat looking at the mountains, trying not to see that cluster of factory chimneys which rolled black fumes above the many-coloured houses. They reminded me of the same abomination on a shore more sacred; from the harbour of Piræus one looks to Athens through trails of coal-smoke.[15] By a contrast pleasant enough, Vesuvius to-day sent forth vapours of a delicate rose-tint, floating far and breaking seaward into soft little fleeces of cirrus. The cone, covered with sulphur, gleamed bright yellow against cloudless blue.

The voyage was resumed at dinner-time; when I came upon deck again, night had fallen. We were somewhere near Sorrento; behind us lay the long curve of faint-glimmering lights on the Naples shore; ahead was Capri. In profound gloom, though under a sky all set with stars, we passed between the island and Cape Minerva; the haven of Capri showed but a faint glimmer; over it towered mighty crags, an awful blackness, a void amid constellations. From my seat near the stern of the vessel I could discern no human form; it was as though I voyaged quite alone in the silence of this magic sea. Silence so all-possessing that the sound of the ship's engine could not reach my ear, but was blended with the water-splash into a lulling murmur. The stillness of a dead world laid its spell on all that lived. To-day seemed an unreality, an idle impertinence; the real was that long-buried past which gave its meaning to all about me, touching the night with infinite pathos. Best of all, one's own being became lost to consciousness; the mind knew only the phantasmal forms it shaped, and was at peace in vision.

2
Paola

I SLEPT little, and was very early on deck, scanning by the light of dawn a mountainous coast. At sunrise I learnt that we were in sight of Paola; as day spread gloriously over earth and sky, the vessel hove to and prepared to land cargo. There, indeed, was the yellowish little town which I had so long pictured; it stood at a considerable height above the shore; harbour there was none at all, only a broad beach of shingle on which waves were breaking, and where a cluster of men, women and children stood gazing at the steamer. It gave me pleasure to find the place so small and primitive. In no hurry to land, I watched the unloading of merchandise (with a great deal of shouting and gesticulation) into boats which had rowed out for the purpose; speculated on the resources of Paola in the matter of food (for I was hungry); and at moments cast an eye towards the mountain barrier which it was probable I should cross to-day.

At last my portmanteau was dropped down on to a laden boat; I, as best I could, managed to follow it; and on the top of a pile of rope and empty flour-sacks we rolled landward. The surf was high; it cost much yelling, leaping, and splashing to gain the dry beach. Meanwhile, not without apprehension, I had eyed the group awaiting our arrival; that they had their eyes on me was obvious, and I knew enough of southern Italians to foresee my reception. I sprang into the midst of a clamorous conflict; half a dozen men were quarrelling for possession of me. No sooner was my luggage on shore than they flung themselves upon it. By what force or authority I know not, one of the fellows triumphed; he turned to me with a satisfied smile, and—presented his wife.

"Mia sposa, signore!"

Wondering, and trying to look pleased, I saw the woman seize the portmanteau (a frightful weight), fling it on to her head, and march away at a good speed. The crowd and I followed to the *dogana*[1], close by, where as rigorous a search was made as I have ever had to undergo. I puzzled the people; my arrival was an unwonted thing, and they felt sure I was a trader of some sort. Dismissed under suspicion, I allowed the lady to whom I had been introduced to guide me townwards. Again she bore the portmanteau on her head, and evidently thought it a trifle, but as the climbing road lengthened, and as I myself began to perspire in the warm sunshine, I looked at my attendant with uncomfortable feelings. It was a long and winding way, but the woman continued to talk and laugh so cheerfully that I tried to forget her toil. At length we reached a cabin where the *dazio* (town dues) officer presented himself, and this conscientious person insisted on making a fresh examination of my baggage; again I explained myself, again I was eyed suspiciously; but he released me, and on we went. I had bidden my guide take me to the best inn; it was the *Leone*[2], a little place which looked from the outside like an ill-kept stable, but was decent enough within. The room into which they showed me had a delightful prospect. Deep beneath the window lay a wild, leafy garden, and lower on the hillside a lemon orchard shining with yellow fruit; beyond, the broad pebbly beach, far seen to north and south, with its white foam edging the blue expanse of sea. There I descried the steamer from which I had landed, just under way for Sicily. The beauty of this view, and the calm splendour of the early morning, put me into happiest mood. After little delay a tolerable breakfast was set before me, with a good rough wine; I ate and drank by the window, exulting in what I saw and all I hoped to see.

Guide-books had informed me that the *corriere* (mail-diligence) from Paola to Cosenza corresponded with the arrival of the Naples steamer, and, after the combat on the beach, my first care was to inquire about this. All and

Entrance to an alley leading to the Piazza del Popolo

sundry made eager reply that the *corriere* had long since gone; that it started, in fact, at 5 A.M., and that the only possible mode of reaching Cosenza that day was to hire a vehicle. Experience of Italian travel made me suspicious, but it afterwards appeared that I had been told the truth. Clearly, if I wished to proceed at once, I must open negotiations at my inn, and, after a leisurely meal, I did so. Very soon a man presented himself who was willing to drive me over the mountains—at a charge which I saw to be absurd; the twinkle in his eye as he named the sum sufficiently enlightened me. By the book it was no more than a journey of four hours; my driver declared that it would take from seven to eight. After a little discussion be accepted half the original demand, and went off very cheerfully to put in his horses.

The Fontana sette canali

For an hour I rambled about the town's one street, very picturesque and rich in colour, with rushing fountains[3] where women drew fair water in jugs and jars of antique beauty. Whilst I was thus loitering in the sunshine, two well-dressed men approached me, and with somewhat excessive courtesy began conversation. They understood that I was about to drive to Cosenza. A delightful day, and a magnificent country! They too thought of journeying to Cosenza, and, in short, would I allow them to share my carriage? Now this was annoying; I much preferred to be alone with my thoughts; but it seemed ungracious to refuse. After a glance at their smiling faces, I answered that whatever room remained in the vehicle was at their service on the natural understanding that they shared the expense; and to this, with the best grace in the world, they at once agreed. We took momentary leave of each other, with much bowing and flourishing of hats, and the amusing thing was that I never beheld those gentlemen again.

Fortunately—as the carriage proved to be a very small one, and the sun was getting very hot; with two companions I should have had an uncomfortable day. In front of the *Leone* a considerable number of loafers had assembled to see me off, and of these some half-dozen were persevering mendicants. It disappointed me that I saw no interesting costume; all wore the common, colourless garb of our destroying age.

The only vivid memory of these people which remains with me is the cadence of their speech. Whilst I was breakfasting, two women stood at gossip on a near balcony, and their utterance was a curious exaggeration of the Neapolitan accent; every sentence rose to a high note, and fell away in a long curve of sound, sometimes a musical wail, more often a mere whining. The protraction of the last word or two was really astonishing; again and again I fancied that the speaker had broken into song. I cannot say that the effect was altogether pleasant; in the end such talk would tell severely on civilized nerves, but it harmonized with the coloured houses, the luxuriant vegetation, the strange odours, the romantic landscape.

In front of the vehicle were three little horses; behind it was hitched an old shabby two-wheeled thing, which we were to leave somewhere for repairs. With whip-cracking and vociferation, amid good-natured farewells from the crowd, we started away. It was just ten o'clock.

At once the road began to climb, and nearly three hours were spent in reaching the highest point of the mountain barrier. Incessantly winding, often doubling upon itself, the road crept up the sides of profound gorges, and skirted many a precipice; bridges innumerable spanned the dry ravines which at another season are filled with furious torrents. From the zone of orange and olive and cactus we passed to that of beech and oak, noble trees now shedding their rich-hued foliage on bracken crisped and brown; here I noticed the feathery bowers of wild clematis ("old man's beard"), and many a spike of the great mullein, strange to me because so familiar in English lanes. Through mists that floated far below I looked over miles of shore, and outward to the ever-rising limit of sea and sky. Very lovely were the effects of light, the gradations of colour; from the blue-black abysses where no shape could be distinguished to those violet hues upon the furrowed heights which had a transparency, a softness, an indefiniteness, unlike anything to be seen in northern landscape.

The driver was accompanied by a half-naked lad, who, at certain points, suddenly disappeared, and came into view again after a few minutes, having made a short cut up some rugged footway between the loops of the road. Perspiring, even as I sat, in the blaze of the sun, I envied the boy his breath and muscle. Now and then he slaked his thirst at a stone fountain by the wayside, not without reverencing the blue-hooded Madonna painted over it. A few lean, brown peasants, bending under faggots, and one or two carts, passed us before we gained the top, and half-way up there was a hovel where drink could be bought; but with these exceptions nothing broke the loneliness of the long, wild ascent. My man was not talkative, but answered inquiries civilly; only on one subject was he very curt—that of the two wooden crosses which we passed just before arriving at the summit; they meant murders. At the moment when I spoke of them I was stretching my legs in a walk beside the carriage, the driver walking just in front of me; and something then happened which is still a puzzle when I recall it. Whether the thought of crimes had made the man nervous, or whether just then I wore a peculiarly truculent face, or had made some alarming gesture, all of a sudden he turned upon me, grasped my arm and asked sharply: "What have you got in your hand?" I had a bit of fern, plucked a few minutes before, and with surprise I showed it; whereupon he murmured an apology, said something about making haste, and jumped to his seat. An odd little incident.

At an unexpected turn of the road there spread before me a vast prospect; I looked down upon inland Calabria. It was a valley broad enough to be called a plain, dotted with white villages, and backed by the mass of mountains which now, as in old time, bear the name of Great Sila. Through this landscape flowed the river Crati—the ancient Crathis; northward it curved, and eastward, to fall at length into the Ionian Sea, far beyond my vision. The river Crathis, which flowed by the walls of Sybaris. I stopped the horses to gaze and wonder; gladly I would have stood there for hours. Less interested, and impatient to get on, the driver pointed out to me the direction of Cosenza, still at a great distance. He added the information that, in summer, the well-to-do folk of Cosenza go to Paola for sea-bathing, and that they always perform the journey by night. I, listening carelessly amid my dream, tried to imagine the crossing of those Calabrian hills under a summer sun! By summer moonlight it must be wonderful.

We descended at a sharp pace, all the way through a forest of chestnuts, the fruit already gathered, the golden leaves rustling in their fall. At the foot lies the village of San Fili, and here we left the crazy old cart which we had dragged so far. A little further, and before us lay a long, level road, a true Roman highway, straight for mile after mile. By this road the Visigoths must have marched after the sack of Rome. In approaching Cosenza I was drawing near to the grave of Alaric. Along this road the barbarian bore in triumph those spoils of the Eternal City which were to enrich his tomb.

By this road, six hundred years before the Goth, marched Hannibal on his sullen retreat from Italy, passing through Consentia to embark at Croton.[4]

3
The Grave of Alaric

IT would have been prudent to consult with my driver as to the inns of Cosenza. But, with a pardonable desire not to seem helpless in his hands, I had from the first directed him to the *Due Lionetti*, relying upon my guide-book.[1] Even at Cosenza there is progress, and guide-books to little-known parts of Europe are easily allowed to fall out of date. On my arrival—

But, first of all, the *dazio*. This time it was a serious business; impossible to convince the rather surly officer that certain of the contents of my portmanteau were not for sale. What in the world was I doing with *tanti libri*?[2] Of course I was a commercial traveller; ridiculous to pretend anything else. After much strain of courtesy, I clapped to my luggage, locked it up, and with resolute face cried "Avanti!" And there was an end of it. In this case, as so often, I have no doubt that simple curiosity went for much in the man's pertinacious questioning. Of course the whole *dazio* business is ludicrous and contemptible; I scarce know a baser spectacle than that of uniformed officials groping in the poor little bundles of starved peasant women, mauling a handful of onions, or prodding with long irons a cartload of straw. Did any one ever compare the expenses with the results?

A glance shows the situation of Cosenza. The town is built on a steep hillside, above the point where two rivers, flowing from the valleys on either side, mingle their waters under one name, that of the Crati. We

The Old Town by the Crati

drove over a bridge which spans the united current, and entered a narrow street, climbing abruptly between houses so high and so close together as to make a gloom amid sunshine. It was four o'clock; I felt tired and half choked with dust; the thought of rest and a meal was very pleasant. As I searched for the sign of my inn, we suddenly drew up, midway in the dark street, before a darker portal, which seemed the entrance to some dirty warehouse, The driver jumped down—"Ecco l'albergo!"

I had seen a good many Italian hostelries, and nourished no unreasonable expectations. The *Lion* at Paola would have seemed to any untravelled Englishman a squalid and comfortless hole, incredible as a place of public entertainment; the *Two Little Lions* of Cosenza made a decidedly worse impression. Over sloppy stones, in an atmosphere heavy with indescribable stenches, I felt rather than saw my way to the foot of a stone staircase; this I ascended, and on the floor above found a dusky room, where tablecloths and an odour of frying oil afforded some suggestion of refreshment.

The arched entrance to the Due Lionetti is on the left

My arrival interested nobody; with a good deal of trouble I persuaded an untidy fellow, who seemed to be a waiter, to come down with me and secure my luggage. More trouble before I could find a bedroom; hunting for keys, wandering up and down stone stairs and along pitch-black corridors, sounds of voices in quarrel. The room itself was utterly depressing—so bare, so grimy, so dark. Quickly I examined the bed, and was rewarded. It is the good point of Italian inns; be the house and the room howsoever sordid, the bed is almost invariably clean and dry and comfortable.

I ate, not amiss; I drank copiously to the memory of Alaric, and felt equal to any fortune. When night had fallen I walked a little about the scarce-lighted streets and came to an open place, dark and solitary and

silent, where I could hear the voices of the two streams as
they mingled below the hill. Presently I passed an open
office of some kind, where a pleasant-looking man sat
at a table writing; on an impulse I entered, and
made bold to ask whether Cosenza had no better
inn than the *Due Lionetti*. Great was this
gentleman's courtesy; he laid down his pen, as if
for ever, and gave himself wholly to my concerns.
His discourse delighted me, so flowing were the
phrases, so rounded the periods. Yes, there were
other inns; one at the top of the town—the
*Vetere*³—in a very good position; and they
doubtless excelled my own in modern comfort. As a
matter of fact, it might be avowed that the *Lionetti*,
from the point of view of the great centres of
civilization, left something to be desired—something to
be desired; but it was a good old inn, a reputable old inn, and
probably on further acquaintance—

Further acquaintance did not increase my respect for the *Lionetti*; it
would not be easy to describe those features in which, most notably, it
fell short of all that might be desired. But I purposed no long stay at
Cosenza, where malarial fever is endemic, and it did not seem worth
while to change my quarters. I slept very well.

I had come here to think about Alaric, and with my own eyes to
behold the place of his burial. Ever since the first boyish reading of
Gibbon, my imagination has loved to play upon that scene of Alaric's
death.⁴ Thinking to conquer Sicily, the Visigoth marched as far as to the
capital of the Bruttii, those mountain tribes which Rome herself never
really subdued; at Consentia he fell sick and died. How often had I
longed to see this river Busento, which the "labour of a captive
multitude" turned aside, that its flood might cover and conceal for all
time the tomb of the Conqueror! I saw it in the light of sunrise, flowing
amid low, brown, olive-planted hills; at this time of the year it is a
narrow, but rapid stream, running through a wide, waste bed of yellow
sand and stones. The Crati, which here has only just started upon its
long seaward way from some glen of Sila, presents much the same

appearance, the track which it has worn in flood being many times as broad as the actual current. They flow, these historic waters, with a pleasant sound, overborne at moments by the clapping noise of Cosenza's washerwomen, who cleanse their linen by beating it, then leave it to dry on the river-bed. Along the banks stood tall poplars, each a spire of burnished gold, blazing against the dark olive foliage on the slopes behind them; plane trees, also, very rich of colour, and fig trees shedding their latest leaves. Now, tradition has it that Alaric was buried close to the confluence of the Busento and the Crati. If so, he lay in full view of the town. But the Goths are said to have slain all their prisoners who took part in the work, to ensure secrecy. Are we to suppose that Consentia was depopulated? On any other supposition the story must be incorrect, and Alaric's tomb would have to be sought at least half a mile away, where the Busento is hidden in its deep valley.

Gibbon, by the way, calls it Busentinus; the true Latin was Buxentius. To make sure of the present name, I questioned some half a dozen peasants, who all named the river Basenzio or Basenz'; a countryman of more intelligent appearance assured me that this was only a dialectical form, the true one being Busento. At a bookseller's shop (Cosenza had one, a very little one[5]) I found the same opinion to prevail.

It is difficult to walk much in this climate; lassitude and feverish symptoms follow on the slightest exertion; but—if one can disregard the evil smells which everywhere catch one's breath—Cosenza has wonders and delights which tempt to day-long rambling. To call the town picturesque is to use an inadequate word; at every step, from the opening of the main street at the hill-foot, up to the stern mediæval castle crowning its height, one marvels and admires. So narrow are the ways that a cart drives the pedestrian into shop or alley; two vehicles (but perhaps the thing never happened) would with difficulty pass each other. As in all towns of Southern Italy, the number of hair-dressers is astonishing, and they hang out the barber's basin—the very basin (of shining brass and with a semicircle cut out of the rim) which the Knight of La Mancha[6] took as substitute for his damaged helmet. Through the gloom of high balconied houses, one climbs to a sunny piazza, where there are several fine buildings; beyond it lies the public garden, a lovely spot, set with alleys of acacia and groups of palm and flower-beds and fountains; marble busts of Garibaldi, Mazzini, and Cavour[7] gleam among the trees. Here one looks down upon the yellow gorge of the Crati, and sees it widen northward into a vast green plain, in which the track of the river is soon lost. On the other side of the Crati valley, in full view of this garden, begins the mountain region of many-folded Sila—a noble sight at any time of the day, but most of all when the mists of morning cling about its summits, or when the sunset clothes its broad flanks with purple. Turn westward, and you behold the long range which hides the Mediterranean; so high and wild from this distance, that I could scarce believe I had driven over it.

Sila—locally the Black Mountain, because dark with climbing forests—held my gaze through a long afternoon. From the grassy table-land of its heights, pasturage for numberless flocks and herds when the long snows have melted, one might look over the shore of the Ionian Sea where Greek craftsmen built ships of timber cut upon the mountain's side. Not so long ago it was a haunt of brigands; now there is no risk for the rare traveller who penetrates that wilderness; but he must needs depend upon the hospitality of labourers and shepherds. I dream of sunny glades, never touched, perhaps, by the foot of man since the Greek herdsman wandered there with his sheep or goats. Somewhere on Sila rises the Neaithos (now Neto) mentioned by Theocritus[8]; one would like to sit by its source in the woodland solitude, and let fancy have her way.

In these garden walks I met a group of peasants, evidently strange to Cosenza, and, wondering at all they saw. The women wore a very striking costume: a short petticoat of scarlet, much embroidered, and over it a blue skirt, rolled up in front and gathered in a sort of knot behind the waist; a bodice adorned with needlework and metal; elaborate glistening head-gear, and bare feet. The town-folk have no peculiarity of dress. I observed among them a grave, intelligent type of countenance, handsome and full of character, which may be that of their brave ancestors the Bruttii. With pleasure I saw that they behaved gently to their beasts, the mules being very sleek and contented-looking.

 There is much difference between these people and the Neapolitans; they seem to have no liking for noise, talk with a certain repose, and allow the stranger to go about among them unmolested, unimportuned. Women above the poorest class are not seen in the streets; there prevails an Oriental system of seclusion.

I was glad to come upon the pot market; in the south of Italy it is always a beautiful and interesting sight. Pottery for commonest use among Calabrian peasants has a grace of line, a charm of colour, far beyond anything native to our most pretentious china-shops. Here still lingers a trace of the old civilization. There must be great good in a people which has preserved this need of beauty through ages of servitude and suffering. Compare such domestic utensils—these oil-jugs and water-jars—with those in the house of an English labourer. Is it really so certain that all virtues of race dwell with those who can rest amid the ugly and know it not for ugliness?

The new age declares itself here and there at Cosenza. A squalid railway station, a hideous railway bridge, have brought the town into the European network; and the craze for building, which has disfigured and half ruined Italy, shows itself in an immense new theatre—Teatro Garibaldi[9]—just being finished. The old one, which stands ruinous close by, struck me as, if anything, too large for the town; possibly it had been damaged by an earthquake, the commonest sort of disaster at Cosenza.[10] On the front of the new edifice I found two inscriptions, both exulting over the fall of the papal power; one was interesting enough to copy:—

20 SETT., 1870.

QUESTA DATA POLITICA
DICE FINITA LA TEOCRAZIA
NEGLI ORDINAMENTI CIVILI.
IL DÌ CHE LA DIRÀ FINITA
MORALMENTE
SARÀ LA DATA UMANA.[11]

*Cosenza: The inscription still in place
on one side of the theatre*

which signifies: "This political date marks the end of theocracy in civil life. The day which ends its moral rule will begin the epoch of humanity." A remarkable utterance anywhere; not least so within hearing of the stream which flows over the grave of Alaric.

One goes to bed early at Cosenza; the night air is dangerous, and—Teatro Garibaldi still incomplete—darkness brings with it no sort of pastime. I did manage to read a little in my miserable room by an antique lamp, but the effort was dispiriting; better to lie in the dark and think of Goth and Roman.

Do the rivers Busento and Crati still keep the secret of that "royal sepulchre, adorned with the splendid spoils and trophies of Rome"?[12] It seems improbable that the grave was ever disturbed; to this day there exists somewhere near Cosenza a treasure-house more alluring than any pictured in Arabian tale. It is not easy to conjecture what "spoils and trophies" the Goths buried with their king; if they sacrificed masses of precious metal, then perchance there still lies in the river-bed some portion of that golden statue of *Virtus*, which the Romans melted down to eke out the ransom claimed by Alaric. The year 410 AD was no unfitting moment to break into bullion the figure personifying Manly Worth. "After that," says an old historian[13], "all bravery and honour perished out of Rome."

4

Taranto

COSENZA is on a line of railway which runs northward up the Crati valley, and joins the long sea-shore line from Taranto to Reggio. As it was my wish to see the whole of that coast, I had the choice of beginning my expedition either at the northern or the southern end; for several reasons I decided to make straight for Taranto.

The train started about seven o'clock in the morning. I rose at six in chill darkness, the discomfort of my room seeming worse than ever at this featureless hour. The waiter—perhaps he was the landlord, I left this doubt unsolved—brought me a cup of coffee; dirtier and more shabbily apparelled man I have never looked upon; viler coffee I never drank. Then I descended into the gloom of the street. The familiar odours breathed upon me with pungent freshness, wafted hither and thither on a mountain breeze. A glance upwards at the narrow strip of sky showed a grey-coloured dawn, prelude, I feared, of a dull day.

Evidently I was not the only traveller departing; on the truck just laden I saw somebody else's luggage, and at the same moment there came forth a man heavily muffled against the air, who, like myself, began to look about for the porter.[1] We exchanged greetings, and on our walk to the station I learned that my companion, also bound for Taranto, had been detained by illness for several days at the *Lionetti*, where, he bitterly complained, the people showed him no sort of attention. He was a commercial traveller, representing a firm of drug merchants in North Italy, and for his sins (as he put it) had to make the southern journey every year; he invariably suffered from fever, and at certain places—of course, the least civilized—had attacks which delayed him from three days to a week. He loathed the South, finding no compensation whatever for the miseries of travel below Naples; the inhabitants he reviled with exceeding animosity. Interested by the doleful predicament of this vendor of drugs (who dosed himself very vigorously), I found him a pleasant companion during the day; after our lunch he seemed to shake off the last shivers of his malady, and was as sprightly an Italian as one could wish to meet—young, sharp-witted, well-mannered, and with a pleasing softness of character.

We lunched at Sybaris; that is to say, at the railway station now so called, though till recently it bore the humbler name of Buffaloria. The Italians are doing their best to revive the classical place-names, where they have been lost, and occasionally the incautious traveller is much misled. Of Sybaris no stone remains above ground; five hundred years before Christ it was destroyed by the people of Croton, who turned the course of the river Crathis so as to whelm the city's ruins. François Lenormant, whose delightful book, *La Grande Grèce*[2], was my companion on this journey, believed that a discovery far more wonderful and important than that of Pompeii awaits the excavator on this site; he held it certain that here, beneath some fifteen feet of alluvial mud, lay the temples and the streets of Sybaris, as on the day when Crathis first flowed over them. A little digging has recently been done, and things of interest have been found; but discovery on a wide scale is still to be attempted.[3]

Lenormant praises the landscape hereabouts as of "incomparable beauty"[4]; unfortunately I saw it on a sunless day, and at unfavourable moments I was strongly reminded of the Essex coast—grey, scrubby flats, crossed by small streams, spreading wearily seaward. One had only to turn inland to correct this mood; the Calabrian mountains, even without sunshine, had their wonted grace. Moreover, cactus and agave, frequent in the foreground, preserved the southern character of the scene. This great plain between the hills and the sea grows very impressive; so silent it is, so mournfully desolate, so haunted with memories of vanished glory. I looked at the Crathis—the Crati of Cosenza—here beginning to spread into a sea-marsh; the waters which used to flow over golden sands, which made white the oxen[5], and sunny-haired the children, that bathed in them, are now lost amid a wilderness poisoned by their own vapours.

The railway station, like all in this region, was set about with eucalyptus. Great bushes of flowering rosemary scented the air, and a fine cassia tree, from which I plucked blossoms, yielded a subtler perfume. Our lunch was not luxurious; I remember only, as at all worthy of Sybaris, a palatable white wine called Moscato dei Saraceni. Appropriate enough amid this vast silence to turn one's thoughts to the Saracens, who are so largely answerable for the ages of desolation that have passed by the Ionian Sea.[6]

Then on for Taranto, where we arrived in the afternoon. Meaning to stay for a week or two I sought a pleasant room in a well-situated hotel, and I found one with a good view of town and harbour.[7] The Taranto of old days, when it was called Taras, or later Tarentum, stood on a long peninsula, which divides a little inland sea from the great sea without. In the Middle Ages the town occupied only the point of this neck of land, which, by the cutting of an artificial channel, had been made into an island: now again it is spreading over the whole of the ancient site; great buildings of yellowish-white stone, as ugly as modern architect can make them, and plainly far in excess of the actual demand for habitations, rise where Phœnicians and Greeks and Romans built after the nobler fashion of their times. One of my windows looked towards the old town, with its long sea-wall where fishermen's nets hung drying, the dome of its Cathedral, the high, squeezed houses, often with gardens on the roofs, and the swing-bridge which links it to the mainland; the other gave me a view across the Mare Piccolo, the Little Sea (it is some twelve miles round about), dotted in many parts with crossed stakes which mark the oyster-beds, and lined on this side with a variety of shipping moored at quays. From some of these vessels, early next

The Mare Piccolo, near the mouth of the Galeso

morning, sounded suddenly a furious cannonade, which threatened to shatter the windows of the hotel; I found it was in honour of the Queen of Italy, whose *festa* fell on that day.[8] This barbarous uproar must have sounded even to the Calabrian heights; it struck me as more meaningless in its deafening volley of noise than any note of joy or triumph that could ever have been heard in old Tarentum.

I walked all round the island part of the town; lost myself amid its maze of streets, or alleys rather, for in many places one could touch both sides with outstretched arms, and rested in the Cathedral of S. Cataldo[9], who, by the bye, was an Irishman. All is strange, but too close-packed to be very striking or beautiful; I found it best to linger on the sea-wall, looking at the two islands in the offing, and over the great gulf with its mountain shore stretching beyond sight. On the rocks below stood fishermen hauling in a great net, whilst a boy splashed the water to drive the fish back until they were safely enveloped in the last meshes; admirable figures, consummate in graceful strength, their bare legs and arms the tone of terra cotta. What slight clothing they wore became them perfectly, as is always the case with a costume well adapted to the natural life of its wearers. Their slow, patient effort speaks of immemorial usage, and is in harmony with time itself. These fishermen are the primitives of Taranto; who shall say for how many centuries they have hauled their nets upon the rock? When Plato visited the Schools of Taras, he saw the same brown-legged figures, in much the same garb, gathering their sea-harvest. When Hannibal, beset by the Romans, drew his ships across the peninsula and so escaped from the inner sea, fishermen of Tarentum went forth as ever, seeking their daily food. A thousand years passed, and the fury of the Saracens, when it had laid the city low, spared some humble Tarentine and the net by which he lived.[10] To-day the fisher-folk form a colony apart; they speak a dialect which retains many Greek words unknown to the rest of the population. I could not gaze at them long enough; their lithe limbs, their attitudes at work or in repose, their wild, black hair, perpetually reminded me of shapes pictured on a classic vase.

Later in the day I came upon a figure scarcely less impressive. Beyond the new quarter of the town, on the ragged edge of its wide, half-peopled streets, lies a tract of olive orchards and of seedland; there, alone amid great bare fields, a countryman was ploughing. The wooden plough, as regards its form, might have been thousands of years old; it was drawn by a little donkey, and traced in the soil—the generous southern soil—the merest scratch of a furrow. I could not but approach the man and exchange words with him; his rude but gentle face, his gnarled hands, his rough and scanty vesture, moved me to a deep respect, and when his speech fell upon my ear, it was as though I listened to one of the ancestors of our kind. Stopping in his work, he answered my inquiries with careful civility; certain phrases escaped me, but on the whole he made himself quite intelligible, and was glad, I could see, when my words proved that I understood him. I drew apart, and watched him again. Never have I seen man so utterly patient, so primævally deliberate. The donkey's method of ploughing was to pull for one minute, and then rest for two; it excited in the ploughman not the least surprise or resentment. Though he held a long stick in his hand, he never made use of it; at each stoppage he contemplated the ass, and then gave utterance to a long "Ah-h-h!" in a note of the most affectionate remonstrance. They were not driver and beast, but comrades in labour. It reposed the mind to look upon them.

Walking onward in the same direction, one approaches a great wall, with gateway sentry-guarded; it is the new Arsenal, the pride of Taranto, and the source of its prosperity. On special as well as on general grounds, I have a grudge against this mass of ugly masonry. I had learnt from Lenormant that at a certain spot, Fontanella[11], by the shore of the Little Sea, were observable great ancient heaps of murex shells—the murex precious for its purple, that of Tarentum yielding in glory only to the purple of Tyre. I hoped to see these shells, perhaps to carry one away. But Fontanella had vanished, swallowed up, with all remnants of antiquity, by the graceless Arsenal. It matters to no one save the few fantastics who hold a memory of the ancient world dearer than any mechanic triumph of to-day. If only one could believe that the Arsenal signified substantial good to Italy! Too plainly it means nothing but the exhaustion of her people in the service of a base ideal.

The confines of this new town being so vague, much trouble is given to that noble institution, the *dazio*. Scattered far and wide in a dusty wilderness, stand the little huts of the officers, vigilant on every road or by-way to wring the wretched soldi from toilsome hands. As became their service, I found these gentry anything but amiable; they had commonly an air of *ennui*, and regarded a stranger with surly suspicion.

When I was back again among the high new houses, my eye, wandering in search of any smallest point of interest, fell on a fresh-painted inscription:—

ALLA MAGNA GRÆCIA.
STABILIMENTO IDROELETTROPATICO.

It was well meant. At the sign of "Magna Græcia" one is willing to accept "hydroelectropathic" as a late echo of Hellenic speech.

François Lenormant (1837–1883)

5
Dulce Galæsi Flumen[1]

TARANTO has a very interesting Museum. I went there with an introduction to the curator[2], who spared no trouble in pointing out to me all that was best worth seeing. He and I were alone in the little galleries; at a second or third visit I had the Museum to myself, save for an attendant who seemed to regard a visitor as a pleasant novelty, and bestirred himself for my comfort when I wanted to make sketches.[3] Nothing is charged for admission, yet no one enters. Presumably, all the Tarentines who care for archæology have already been here, and strangers are few.

Upon the shelves are seen innumerable miniature busts, carved in some kind of stone; thought to be simply portraits of private persons. One peers into the faces of men, women, and children, vaguely conjecturing their date, their circumstances; some of them may have

dwelt in the old time on this very spot of ground now covered by the Museum. Like other people who grow too rich and comfortable, the citizens of Tarentum loved mirth and mockery; their Greek theatre was remarkable for irreverent farce, for parodies of the great drama of Athens. And here is testimony to the fact: all manner of comic masks, of grotesque visages; mouths distorted into impossible grins, eyes leering and goggling, noses extravagant. I sketched a caricature of Medusa, the anguished features and snaky locks travestied with satiric grimness. You

remember a story which illustrates this scoffing habit: how the Roman Ambassador, whose Greek left something to be desired, excited the uproarious derision of the assembled Tarentines—with results which were no laughing matter.[4]

I used the opportunity of my conversation with the Director of the Museum to ask his aid in discovering the river Galæsus. Who could find himself at Taranto without turning in thought to the Galæsus, and wishing to walk along its banks? Unhappily, one cannot be quite sure of its position. A stream there is, flowing into the Little Sea, which by some is called Galeso; but the country-folk commonly give it the name of Gialtrezze. Of course I turned my steps in that direction, to see and judge for myself.

To skirt the western shore of the Mare Piccolo I had to pass the railway station, and there I made a few inquiries; the official with whom

I spoke knew not the name Galeso, but informed me that the Gialtrezze entered the sea at a distance of some three kilometres. That I purposed walking such a distance to see an insignificant stream excited the surprise, even the friendly concern, of my interlocutor; again and again he assured me it was not worth while, repeating emphatically, "*Non c'è novità.*"[5] But I went my foolish way. Of two or three peasants or fishermen on the road I asked the name of the little river I was approaching; they answered, "Gialtrezze". Then came a man carrying a gun, whose smile and greeting invited question. "Can you tell me the name of the stream which flows into the sea just beyond here?" "Signore, it is the Galeso."

My pulse quickened with delight; all the more when I found that my informant had no tincture of the classics, and that he supported Galeso against Gialtrezze simply as a question of local interest. Joyously I took leave of him, and very soon I was in sight of the river itself. The river? It is barely half a mile long; it rises amid a bed of great reeds, which quite conceal the water, and flows with an average breadth of some ten feet down to the seashore, on either side of it bare, dusty fields, and. a few hoary olives.

The Galæsus?—the river beloved by Horace; its banks pasturing a famous breed of sheep, with fleece so precious that it was protected by a garment of skins? Certain it is that all the waters of Magna Græcia have much diminished since classic times, but (unless there have been great local changes, due, for example, to an earthquake) this brook had always

The Galeso flowing into the Mare Piccolo

A typical alley in the Old Town

the same length, and it is hard to think of the Galæsus as so insignificant. Disappointed, brooding, I followed the current seaward, and upon the shore, amid scents of mint and rosemary, sat down to rest.

There was a good view of Taranto across the water; the old town on its little island, compact of white houses, contrasting with the yellowish tints of the great new buildings which spread over the peninsula. With half-closed eyes, one could imagine the true Tarentum. Wavelets lapped upon the sand before me, their music the same as two thousand years ago. A goatherd came along, his flock straggling behind him; man and goats were as much of the old world as of the new. Far away, the boats of fishermen floated silently. I heard a rustle as an old fig tree hard by dropped its latest leaves. On the sea-bank of yellow crumbling earth lizards flashed about me in the sunshine. After a dull morning, the day had passed into golden serenity; a stillness as of eternal peace held earth and sky.

"Dearest of all to me is that nook of earth which yields not to Hymettus for its honey, nor for its olive to green Venafrum; where heaven grants a long springtime and warmth in winter, and in the sunny hollows Bacchus fosters a vintage noble as the Falernian—"6 The lines of Horace sang in my head; I thought, too, of the praise of Virgil, who, tradition has it, wrote his *Eclogues* hereabouts. Of course, the country has another aspect in spring and early summer; I saw it at a sad moment; but, all allowance made for seasons, it is still with wonder that one recalls the rapture of the poets. A change beyond conception must have come upon these shores of the Ionian Sea. The scent of rosemary seemed to be wafted across the ages from a vanished world.

After all, who knows whether I have seen the Galæsus? Perhaps, as some hold, it is quite another river, flowing far to the west of Taranto into the open gulf. Gialtrezze may have become Galeso merely because of the desire in scholars to believe that it was the classic stream; in other parts of Italy names have been so imposed. But I shall not give ear to such discouraging argument. It is little likely that my search will ever be renewed, and for me the Galæsus—"dulce Galæsi flumen"—is the stream I found and tracked, whose waters I heard mingle with the Little Sea. The memory has no sense of disappointment. Those reeds which rustle about the hidden source seem to me fit shelter of a Naiad; I am glad I could not see the water bubbling in its spring, for there remains a mystery. Whilst I live, the Galæsus purls and glistens in the light of that golden afternoon, and there beyond, across the blue still depths, glimmers a vision of Tarentum.

Let Taranto try as it will to be modern and progressive, there is a retarding force which shows little sign of being overcome—the profound superstition of the people. A striking episode of street life[7] reminded me how near akin were the southern Italians of to-day to their predecessors in what are called the dark ages; nay, to those more illustrious ancestors who were so ready to believe that an ox had uttered an oracle, or that a stone had shed blood. Somewhere near the swing-bridge, where undeniable steamships go and come between the inner and the outer sea, I saw a crowd gathered about a man who was exhibiting a picture and expounding its purport; every other minute the male listeners doffed their hats, the females bowed and crossed themselves. When I had pressed near enough to hear the speaker, I found he was just finishing a wonderful story, in which he himself might or might not have faith, but which plainly commanded the credit of his auditors. Having closed his narrative, the fellow began to sell it in printed form—little pamphlets with a rude illustration on the cover. I bought the thing for a soldo, and read it as I walked away.

A few days ago—thus, after a pious exordium, the relation began—in that part of Italy called Marca, there came into a railway station a Capuchin friar of grave, thoughtful, melancholy aspect, who besought the station-master to allow him to go without ticket by the train just starting, as he greatly desired to reach the Sanctuary of Loreto that day, and had no money to pay his fare. The official gave a contemptuous refusal, and paid no heed to the entreaties of the friar, who urged all manner of religious motives for the granting of his request. The two engines on the train (which was a very long one) seemed about to steam away—but, behold, con *grande stupore di tutti* [8], the waggons moved not at all! Presently a third engine was put on, but still all efforts to start the train proved useless. Alone of the people who viewed this inexplicable event, the friar showed no astonishment; he remarked calmly, that so long as he was refused permission to travel by it, the train would not stir. At length *un ricco signore* [9] found a way out of the difficulty by purchasing the friar a third-class ticket; with a grave reproof to the station-master, the friar took his seat, and the train went its way.

But the matter, of course, did not end here. Indignant and amazed, and wishing to be revenged upon that *frataccio* [10], the station-master telegraphed to Loreto, that in a certain carriage of a certain train was travelling a friar, whom it behoved the authorities to arrest for having hindered the departure of the said train for fifteen minutes, and also for the offence of mendicancy within a railway station. Accordingly, the Loreto police sought the offender, but, in the compartment where he had travelled, found no person; there, however, lay a letter couched in these terms: "He who was in this waggon under the guise of a humble friar, has now ascended into the arms of his *Santissima Madre Maria*. He wished to make known to the world how easy it is for him to crush the pride of unbelievers, or to reward those who respect religion."

Nothing more was discoverable; wherefore the learned of the Church—*i dotti della chiesa*—came to the conclusion that under the guise of a friar there had actually appeared "N. S. G. C." [11] The Supreme Pontiff and his prelates had not yet delivered judgment in the matter, but there could be no sort of doubt that they would pronounce the authenticity of the miracle. With a general assurance that the good Christian will be saved and the unrepentant will be damned, this remarkable little pamphlet came to an end. Much verbiage I have omitted, but the translation, as far as it goes, is literal. Doubtless many a humble Tarentine spelt it through that evening, with boundless wonder, and thought such an intervention of Providence worthy of being talked about, until the next stabbing case in his street provided a more interesting topic.

Possibly some malevolent rationalist might note that the name of the railway station where this miracle befell was nowhere mentioned. Was it not open to him to go and make inquiries at Loreto?

6

The Table of the Paladins

FOR two or three days a roaring north wind whitened the sea with foam; it kept the sky clear, and from morning to night there was magnificent sunshine, but, none the less, one suffered a good deal from cold. The streets were barer than ever; only in the old town, where high, close walls afforded a good deal of shelter, was there a semblance of active life. But even here most of the shops seemed to have little, if any, business; frequently I saw the tradesman asleep in a chair, at any hour of daylight. Indeed, it must be very difficult to make the day pass at Taranto. I noticed that, as one goes southward in Italy, the later do ordinary people dine: appetite comes slowly in this climate. Between *colazione* at midday and *pranzo* at eight, or even half-past, what an abysm of time! Of course, the Tarentine never reads; the only bookshop I could discover made a poorer display than even that at Cosenza—it was not truly a bookseller's at all, but a fancy stationer's. How the women spend their lives one may vainly conjecture. Only on Sunday did I see a few of them about the street; they walked to and from Mass, with eyes on the ground, and all the better-dressed of them wore black.

When the weather fell calm again, and there was pleasure in walking, I chanced upon a trace of the old civilization which interested me more than objects ranged in a museum. Rambling eastward along the outer shore, in the wilderness which begins as soon as the town has disappeared, I came to a spot as uninviting as could be imagined, great mounds of dry rubbish, evidently deposited here by the dust-carts of Taranto; luckily, I continued my walk beyond this obstacle, and after a while became aware that I had entered upon a road—a short piece of well-marked road, which began and ended in the mere waste. A moment's examination, and I saw that it was no modern by-way. The track was clean-cut in living rock, its smooth, hard surface lined with two parallel ruts nearly a foot deep; it extended for some twenty yards without a break, and further on I discovered less perfect bits. Here, manifestly, was the seaside approach to Tarentum, to Taras, perhaps to the Phœnician city which came before them. Ages must have passed since vehicles used this way; the modern high road is at some distance inland, and one sees at a glance that this witness of ancient traffic has remained by Time's sufferance in a desert region. Wonderful was the preservation of the surface: the angles at the sides, where the road had been cut down a little below the rock-level, were sharp and clean as if carved yesterday, and the profound ruts, worn, perhaps, before Rome had come to her power, showed the grinding of wheels with strange distinctness. From this point there is an admirable view of Taranto, the sea, and the mountains behind.

Of the ancient town there remains hardly anything worthy of being called a ruin. Near the shore, however, one can see a few remnants of a theatre—perhaps that theatre where the Tarentines were sitting when they saw Roman galleys, in scorn of treaty, sailing up the Gulf.[1]

My last evenings were brightened by very beautiful sunsets; one in particular remains with me; I watched it for an hour or more from the terrace-road of the island town. An exquisite after-glow seemed as if it would never pass away. Above, thin, grey clouds stretching along the horizon a purple flush melted insensibly into the dark blue of the zenith. Eastward the sky was piled with lurid rack, sullen-tinted folds edged with the hue of sulphur. The sea had a strange aspect, curved tracts of pale blue lying motionless upon a dark expanse rippled by the wind. Below me, as I leaned on the sea-wall, a fisherman's boat crept duskily along the rocks, a splash of oars soft-sounding in the stillness. I looked to the far Calabrian hills, now scarce distinguishable from horizon cloud, and wondered what chances might await me in the unknown scenes of my further travel.

The long shore of the Ionian Sea suggested many a halting-place. Best of all, I should have liked to swing a wallet on my shoulder and make the whole journey on foot; but this for many reasons was impossible. I could only mark points of the railway where some sort of food or lodging might be hoped for, and the first of these stoppages was Metaponto.

Official time-bills of the month marked a train for Metaponto at 4.56 A.M., and this I decided to take, as it seemed probable that I might find a stay of some hours sufficient, and so be able to resume my journey before night. I asked the waiter to call me at a quarter to four. In the middle of the night (as it seemed to me) I was aroused by a knocking, and the waiter's voice called to me that, if I wished to leave early for Metaponto, I had better get up at once, as the departure of the train had been changed to 4.15—it was now half-past three. There ensued an argument, sustained, on my side, rather by the desire to stay in bed this cold morning than by any faith in the reasonableness of the railway company. There must be a mistake! The *orario* for the month gave 4.56, and how could the time of a train be changed without public notice? Changed it was, insisted the waiter; it had happened a few days ago, and they had only heard of it at the hotel this very morning. Angry and uncomfortable, I got my clothes on, and drove to the station, where I found that a sudden change in the time-table, without any regard for persons relying upon the official guide, was taken as a matter of course. In chilly darkness I bade farewell to Taranto.

At a little after six, when palest dawn was shimmering on the sea, I found myself at Metaponto, with no possibility of doing anything for a couple of hours. Metaponto is a railway station, that and nothing more, and, as the station also calls itself a hotel, I straightway asked for a room, and there dozed until sunshine improved my humour and stirred my appetite. The guide-book had assured me of two things: that a vehicle could be had here for surveying the district[2], and that, under cover behind the station, one would find a little collection of antiquities unearthed hereabout. On inquiry, I found that no vehicle, and no animal capable of being ridden, existed at Metaponto; also that the little museum had been transferred to Naples. It did not pay to keep the horse, they told me; a stranger asked for it only "once in a hundred years". However, a lad was forthcoming who would guide me to the ruins. I breakfasted (the only thing tolerable being the wine), and we set forth.

It was a walk of some two or three miles, by a cart road, through fields just being ploughed for grain. All about lay a level or slightly rolling country, which in winter becomes a wilderness of mud; dry traces of vast slough and occasional stagnant pools showed what the state of things would be a couple of months hence. The properties were divided by hedges of agave—huge growths, grandly curving their sword-pointed leaves. Its companion, the spiny cactus, writhed here and there among juniper bushes and tamarisks. Along the wayside rose tall, dead thistles, white with age, their great cluster of seed-vessels showing how fine the flower had been. Above our heads, peewits were wheeling and crying, and lizards swarmed on the hard, cracked ground.

We passed a few ploughmen, with white oxen yoked to labour. Ploughing was a fit sight at Metapontum, famous of old for the richness of its soil; in token whereof the city dedicated at Delphi its famous Golden Sheaf.[3] It is all that remains of life on this part of the coast; the city had sunk into ruin before the Christian era, and was never rebuilt. Later, the shore was too dangerous for habitation. Of all the cities upon the Ionian Sea, only Tarentum and Croton continued to exist through

The Table of the Paladins

the Middle Ages, for they alone occupied a position strong for defence
against pirates and invaders. A memory of the Saracen wars lingers in
the name borne by the one important relic of Metapontum, the *Tavola
de' Paladini*; to this my guide was conducting me.[4]

It is the ruin of a temple to an unknown god, which stood at some
distance north of the ancient city; two parallel rows of columns, ten on
one side, five on the other, with architrave all but entire, and a basement
shattered. The fine Doric capitals are well preserved; the pillars
themselves, crumbling under the tooth of time, seem to support with
difficulty their noble heads. This monument must formerly have been
very impressive amid the wide landscape; but, a few years ago, for
protection against peasant depredators, a wall ten feet high was built
close around the columns, so that no good view of them is any longer
obtainable. To the enclosure admission is obtained through an iron
gateway with a lock. I may add, as a picturesque detail, that the lock has
long been useless; my guide simply pushed the gate open. Thus, the ugly
wall serves no purpose whatever save to detract from the beauty of the
scene.[5]

Vegetation is thick within the temple precincts; a flowering rose bush made contrast of its fresh and graceful loveliness with the age-worn strength of these great carved stones. About their base grew luxuriantly a plant which turned my thoughts for a moment to rural England, the round-leaved pennywort. As I lingered here, there stirred in me something of that deep emotion which I felt years ago amid the temples of Paestum.[6] Of course, this obstructed fragment holds no claim to comparison with Paestum's unique glory, but here, as there, one is possessed by the pathos of immemorial desolation; amid a silence which the voice has no power to break, nature's eternal vitality triumphs over the greatness of forgotten men.

At a distance of some three miles from this temple there lies a little lake, or a large pond, which would empty itself into the sea but for a piled barrier of sand and shingle. This was the harbour of Metapontum.[7]

I passed the day in rambling and idling, and returned for a meal at the station just before train-time. The weather could not have been more enjoyable; a soft breeze and cloudless blue. For the last half-hour I lay in a hidden corner of the eucalyptus grove trying to shape in fancy some figure of old Pythagoras.[8] He died here (says story) in 497 BC— broken-hearted at the failure of his efforts to make mankind gentle and reasonable. In 1897 AD that hope had not come much nearer to its realization.[9] Italians are yet familiar with the name of the philosopher, for it is attached to the multiplication table, which they call *tavola pitagorica.* What, in truth, do we know of him? He is a type of aspiring humanity; a sweet and noble figure, moving as a dim radiance through legendary Hellas. The English reader hears his name with a smile, recalling only the mention of him, in mellow mirth, by England's greatest spirit. "What is the opinion of Pythagoras concerning wild fowl?" Whereto replies the much-offended Malvolio: "That the soul of our grandam might haply inhabit a bird." He of the crossed garters disdains such fantasy. "I think nobly of the soul, and no way approve his opinion."[10]

I took my ticket for Cotrone, which once was Croton. At Croton, Pythagoras enjoyed his moment's triumph, ruling men to their own behoof. At Croton grew up a school of medicine which glorified Magna Græcia. "Healthier than Croton", said a proverb[11]; for the spot was unsurpassed in salubrity; beauty and strength distinguished its inhabitants, who boasted their champion Milon.[12] After the fall of Sybaris, Croton became so populous that its walls encircled twelve miles. Hither came Zeuxis[13], to adorn with paintings the great temple of Hera on the Lacinian promontory; here he made his picture of Helen, with models chosen from the loveliest maidens of the city. I was light-hearted with curious anticipation as I entered the train for Cotrone.

While daylight lasted, the moving landscape held me attentive. This part of the coast is more varied, more impressive, than that between Taranto and Metaponto. For the most part a shaggy wilderness, the ground lies in strangely broken undulations, much hidden with shrub and tangled boscage. At the falling of dusk we passed a thickly wooded tract large enough to be called a forest; the great trees looked hoary with age, and amid a jungle of undergrowth, myrtle and lentisk, arbutus and oleander, lay green marshes, dull deep pools, sluggish streams. A spell which was half fear fell upon the imagination; never till now had I known an enchanted wood. Nothing human could wander in those pathless shades, by those dead waters. It was the very approach to the world of spirits; over this woodland, seen on the verge of twilight, brooded a silent awe, such as Dante knew in his *selva oscura*.[14]

Of a sudden the dense foliage was cleft; there opened a broad alley between drooping boughs, and in the deep hollow, bordered with sand and stones, a flood rolled seaward. This river is now called Sinno; it was the ancient Siris, whereon stood the city of the same name.[15] In the seventh century before Christ, Siris was lauded as the richest city in the world; for luxury it outrivalled Sybaris.

I had recently been reading Lenormant's description of the costumes of Magna Græcia prior to the Persian wars.[16] Siris, a colony from Ionia, still kept its Oriental style of dress. Picture a man in a long, close-clinging tunic which descended to his feet, either of fine linen, starched and pleated, or of wool, falling foldless, enriched with embroidery and adorned with bands of gay-coloured geometric patterns; over this a wrap (one may say) of thick wool, tight round the bust and leaving the right arm uncovered, or else a more ample garment, elaborately decorated like the long tunic. Complete the picture with a head ornately dressed, on the brow a fringe of ringlets; the long hair behind held together by gold wire spirally wound; above, a crowning fillet, with a jewel set in the front; the beard cut to a point, and the upper lip shaven. You behold the citizen of these Hellenic colonies in their stately prime.

Somewhere in that enchanted forest, where the wild vine trails from tree to tree, where birds and creatures of the marshy solitude haunt their ancient home, lie buried the stones of Siris.

7

Cotrone

NIGHT hid from me the scenes that followed. Darkling, I passed again through the station called Sybaris, and on and on by the sea-shore, the sound of breakers often audible. From time to time I discerned black mountain masses against a patch of grey sky, or caught a glimpse of blanching wave, or felt my fancy thrill as a stray gleam from the engine fire revealed for a moment another trackless wood. Often the hollow rumbling of the train told me that we were crossing a bridge; the stream beneath it bore, perhaps, a name in legend or in history. A wind was rising; at the dim little stations I heard it moan and buffet, and my carriage, where all through the journey I sat alone, seemed the more comfortable. Rain began to fall, and when, about ten o'clock, I alighted at Cotrone, the night was loud with storm.

There was but one vehicle at the station, a shabby, creaking, mud-plastered sort of coach, into which I bundled together with two travellers of the kind called commercial—almost the only species of traveller I came across during these southern wanderings. A long time was spent in stowing freightage which, after all, amounted to very little; twice, thrice, four, and perhaps five times did we make a false start, followed by uproarious vociferation, and a jerk which tumbled us passengers all together. The gentlemen of commerce rose to wild excitement, and roundly abused the driver; as soon as we really started, their wrath changed to boisterous gaiety. On we rolled, pitching and tossing, mid darkness and tempest, until, through the broken window, a sorry illumination of oil-lamps showed us one side of a colonnaded street. "Bologna! Bologna!"[1] cried my companions, mocking at this feeble reminiscence of their fat northern town. The next moment we pulled up, our bruised bodies colliding vigorously for the last time; it was the *Albergo Concordia.*[2]

The Arcades, Piazza Vittoria, c. 1900. The Albergo Concordia, now Italia, is at bottom right

A dark stone staircase, yawning under the colonnade; on the first landing an open doorway; within, a long corridor, doors of bedrooms on either side, and in a room at the far end a glimpse of a tablecloth. This was the hotel, the whole of it.[3] As soon as I grasped the situation, it was clear to me why my fellow travellers had entered with a rush, and flung themselves into rooms; there might, perchance, be only one or two chambers vacant, and I knew already that Cotrone offered no other decent harbourage.[4] Happily I did not suffer for my lack of experience; after trying one or two doors in vain, I found a sleeping-place which seemed to be unoccupied, and straightway took possession of it. No one appeared to receive the arriving guests. Feeling very hungry, I went into the room at the end of the passage, where I had seen a tablecloth; a wretched lamp burned on the wall, but only after knocking, stamping, and calling did I attract attention; then issued from some mysterious region a stout, slatternly, sleepy woman, who seemed surprised at my demand for food, but at length complied with it. I was to have better acquaintance with my hostess of the *Concordia* before I quitted Cotrone.[5]

Next morning the wind still blew, but the rain was over; I could begin my rambles. Like the old town of Taranto, Cotrone occupies the site of the ancient acropolis, a little headland jutting into the sea; above, and in front of the town itself, stands the castle built by Charles V[6], with immense battlements looking over the harbour. From a road skirting the shore around the base of the fortress one views a wide bay, bounded to the north by the dark flanks of Sila (I was in sight of the Black Mountain once more), and southwards by a long low promontory, its level slowly declining to the far-off point where it ends amid the waves. On this Cape I fixed my eyes, straining them until it seemed to me that I distinguished something, a jutting speck against the sky, at its farthest point. Then I used my field-glass[7], and at once the doubtful speck became a clearly visible projection, much like a lighthouse. It is a Doric column, some five-and-twenty feet high; the one pillar that remains of the great temple of Hera, renowned through all the Hellenic world, and sacred still when the goddess had for centuries borne a Latin name. "Colonna" is the ordinary name of the Cape; but it is also known as *Capo di Naù*, a name which preserves the Greek word *naos* (temple).

I planned for the morrow a visit to this spot, which is best reached by sea. To-day great breakers were rolling upon the strand, and all the blue of the bay was dashed with white foam; another night would, I hoped, bring calm, and then the voyage! *Dis aliter visum.*[8]

A little fleet of sailing vessels and coasting steamers had taken refuge within the harbour, which is protected by a great mole. A good haven; the only one, indeed, between Taranto and Reggio, but it grieves one to remember that the mighty blocks built into the sea-barrier came from that fallen temple. We are told that as late as the sixteenth century the

The remaining column of the temple of Hera on Capo Colonna

building remained all but perfect, with eight-and-forty pillars, rising there above the Ionian Sea; a guide to sailors, even as when Æneas marked it on his storm-tossed galley.[9] Then it was assailed, cast down, ravaged by a Bishop of Cotrone, one Antonio Lucifero, to build his episcopal palace. Nearly three hundred years later, after the terrible earthquake of 1783, Cotrone strengthened her harbour with the great stones of the temple basement. It was a more legitimate pillage.

Driven inland by the gale, I wandered among low hills which overlook the town. Their aspect is very strange, for they consist entirely—on the surface, at all events—of a yellowish-grey mud, dried hard, and as bare as the high road. A few yellow hawkweeds, a few camomiles, grew in hollows here and there; but of grass not a blade. It is easy to make a model of these Crotonian hills. Shape a solid mound of hard-pressed sand, and then, from the height of a foot or two, let water trickle down upon it; the perpendicular ridges and furrows thus formed upon the miniature hill represent exactly what I saw here on a larger scale. Moreover, all the face of the ground is minutely cracked and wrinkled; a square foot includes an incalculable multitude of such meshes. Evidently this is the work of hot sun on moisture; but when was it done? For they tell me that it rains very little at Cotrone, and only a deluge could moisten this iron soil. Here and there I came upon yet more striking evidences of water-power; great holes on the hillside, generally funnel-shaped, and often deep enough to be dangerous to the careless walker. The hills are round-topped, and parted one from another by gully or ravine, shaped, one cannot but think, by furious torrents. A desolate landscape, and scarcely bettered when one turned to look over the level which spreads north of the town; one discovers patches of foliage, indeed, the dark perennial verdure of the south; but no kindly herb clothes the soil. In springtime, it seems, there is a growth of grass, very brief, but luxuriant. That can only be on the lower ground; these furrowed heights declare a perpetual sterility.

What has become of the ruins of Croton? This squalid little town of to-day has nothing left from antiquity. Yet a city bounded with a wall of twelve miles circumference is not easily swept from the face of the earth. Bishop Lucifer, wanting stones for his palace, had to go as far as the Cape Colonna; then, as now, no block of Croton remained. Nearly two hundred years before Christ the place was forsaken. Rome colonized it anew, and it recovered an obscure life as a place of embarkation for Greece, its houses occupying only the rock of the ancient citadel. Were there at that date any remnants of the great Greek city?—still great only two centuries before. Did all go to the building of Roman dwellings and temples and walls, which since have crumbled or been buried?

We are told that the river Æsarus flowed through the heart of the city at its prime.[10] I looked over the plain, and yonder, towards the distant railway station, I descried a green track, the course of the all but stagnant and wholly pestilential stream, still called Esaro. Near its marshy mouth are wide orange orchards. Could one but see in vision the harbour, the streets, the vast encompassing wall! From the eminence where I stood, how many a friend and foe of Croton has looked down upon its shining ways, peopled with strength and beauty and wisdom! Here Pythagoras may have walked, glancing afar at the Lacinian sanctuary, then new built.

Lenormant is eloquent on the orange groves of Cotrone.[11] In order to visit them, permission was necessary, and presently I made my way to the town hall, to speak with the Sindaco (Mayor) and request his aid in this matter. Without difficulty I was admitted. In a well-furnished office sat two stout gentlemen, smoking cigars, very much at their ease; the Sindaco[12] bade me take a chair, and scrutinized me with doubtful curiosity as I declared my business. Yes, to be sure he could admit me to see his own orchard; but why did I wish to see it? My reply that I had no interest save in the natural beauty of the place did not convince him; he saw in me a speculator of some kind. That was natural enough. In all the south of Italy, money is the one subject of men's thoughts; intellectual life does not exist; there is little even of what we should call common education. Those who have wealth cling to it fiercely; the majority have neither time nor inclination to occupy themselves with anything but the earning of a livelihood which for multitudes signifies the bare appeasing of hunger.

Seeing the Sindaco's embarrassment, his portly friend began to question me; good-humouredly enough, but in such a fat bubbling voice (made more indistinct by the cigar he kept in his mouth) that with difficulty I understood him. What was I doing at Cotrone? I endeavoured to explain that Cotrone greatly interested me. Ha! Cotrone interested me? Really? Now what did I find interesting at Cotrone? I spoke of historic associations. The Sindaco and his friend exchanged glances, smiled in a puzzled, tolerant, half-pitying way, and decided that my request might be granted. In another minute I withdrew, carrying half a sheet of note-paper on which were scrawled in pencil a few words, followed by the proud signature "Berlingieri". When I had deciphered the scrawl, I found it was an injunction to allow me to view a certain estate "*senza nulla toccare*"—without touching anything. So a doubt still lingered in the dignitary's mind.

Cotrone has no vehicle plying for hire—save that in which I arrived at the hotel. I had to walk in search of the orange orchard, all along the straight dusty road leading to the station. For a considerable distance this road is bordered on both sides by warehouses of singular appearance. They have only a ground floor, and the front wall is not more than ten feet high, but their low roofs, sloping to the ridge at an angle of about thirty degrees, cover a great space. The windows are strongly barred, and the doors show immense padlocks of elaborate construction. The goods warehoused here are chiefly wine and oil, oranges and liquorice.[13] (A great deal of liquorice grows around the southern gulf.) At certain moments, indicated by the markets at home or abroad, these stores are conveyed to the harbour, and shipped away. For the greater part of the year the houses stand as I saw them, locked, barred, and forsaken: a street where any sign of life is exceptional; an odd suggestion of the English Sunday in a land that knows not such observance.

Crossing the Esaro, I lingered on the bridge to gaze at its green, muddy water, not visibly flowing at all. The high reeds which half concealed it carried my thoughts back to the Galæsus. But the comparison is all in favour of the Tarentine stream. Here one could feel nothing but a comfortless melancholy; the scene is too squalid, the degradation too complete.

Of course, no one looked at the *permesso* with which I presented myself at the entrance to the orchard. From a tumbling house, which we should call the lodge, came forth (after much shouting on my part) an aged woman, who laughed at the idea that she should be asked to read anything, and bade me walk wherever I liked. I strayed at pleasure, meeting only a lean dog, which ran fearfully away. The plantation was very picturesque; orange trees by no means occupied all the ground, but mingled with pomegranates and tamarisks and many evergreen shrubs of which I knew not the name; whilst here and there soared a magnificent stone pine. The walks were bordered with giant cactus, now and again so fantastic in their growth that I stood to wonder; and in an open space upon the bank of the Esaro (which stagnates through the orchard) rose a majestic palm, its leaves stirring heavily in the wind which swept above. Picturesque, abundantly; but these beautiful tree-names, which waft a perfume of romance, are like to convey a false impression to readers who have never seen the far South; it is natural to think of lovely nooks, where one might lie down to rest and dream; there comes a vision of soft turf under the golden-fruited boughs—"places of nestling green for poets made."[14] Alas! the soil is bare and lumpy as a ploughed field, and all the leafage that hangs low is thick with a clayey dust. One cannot rest or loiter or drowse; no spot in all the groves where by any possibility one could sit down. After rambling as long as I chose, I found that a view of the orchard from outside was more striking than the picture amid the trees themselves. *Senza nulla toccare*, I went my way.

8
Faces By the Way

THE wind could not roar itself out. Through the night it kept awaking me, and on the morrow I found a sea foamier than ever; impossible to reach the Colonna by boat, and almost so, I was assured, to make the journey by land in such weather as this. Perforce I waited.

A cloudless sky; broad sunshine, warm as in an English summer; but the roaring *tramontana* was disagreeably chill. No weather could be more perilous to health. The people of Cotrone, those few of them who did not stay at home or shelter in the porticoes, went about heavily cloaked, and I wondered at their ability to wear such garments under so hot a sun. Theoretically aware of the danger I was running, but, in fact, thinking little about it, I braved the wind and the sunshine all day long; my sketch-book gained by it, and my store of memories.

First of all, I looked into the Cathedral, an ugly edifice, as uninteresting within as without. Like all the churches in Calabria, it is whitewashed from door to altar, pillars no less than walls—a cold and depressing interior. I could see no picture of the least merit; one, a figure of Christ with hideous wounds, was well-nigh as repulsive as painting could be. This vile realism seems to indicate Spanish influence. There is a miniature copy in bronze of the statue of the chief Apostle in St. Peter's at Rome, and beneath it an inscription making known to the faithful that, by order of Leo XIII in 1896, an Indulgence of three hundred days is granted to whosoever kisses the bronze toe and says a prayer. Familiar enough this unpretentious announcement, yet it never fails of its little shock to the heretic mind. Whilst I was standing near, a peasant went through the mystic rite; to judge from his poor malaria-stricken countenance, he prayed very earnestly, and I hope his Indulgence benefited him. Probably he repeated a mere formula learnt by heart. I wished he could have prayed spontaneously for three hundred days of wholesome and sufficient food, and for as many years of honest, capable government in his heavy-burdened country.

When travelling, I always visit the burial-ground[1]; I like to see how a people commemorates its dead, for tombstones have much significance. The cemetery of Cotrone lies by the sea-shore, at some distance beyond the port, far away from habitations; a bare hillside looks down upon its graves, and the road which goes by is that leading to Cape Colonna. On the way I passed a little ruined church, shattered, I was told, by an earthquake three years before; its lonely position made it interesting, and the cupola of coloured tiles (like that of the Cathedral at Amalfi) remained intact, a bright spot against the grey hills behind. A high enclosing wall signalled the cemetery; I rang a bell at the gate and was admitted by a man of behaviour and language much more refined than is common among the people of this region[2]; I felt sorry, indeed, that I had not found him seated in the Sindaco's chair that morning. But as guide to the burial-ground he was delightful. Nine years, he told me, he had held the post of custodian, in which time, working with his own hands, and unaided, he had turned the enclosure from a wretched wilderness into a beautiful garden. Unaffectedly I admired the results of his labour, and my praise rejoiced him greatly. He specially requested me

Giulio Marino,
custodian and gardener of the Cotrone cemetery

to observe the geraniums; there were ten species, many of them of extraordinary size and with magnificent blossoms. Roses I saw, too, in great abundance; and tall snapdragons, and bushes of rosemary, and many flowers unknown to me. As our talk proceeded the gardener gave me a little light on his own history; formerly he was valet to a gentleman of Cotrone, with whom he had travelled far and wide over Europe[3]; yes, even to London, of which he spoke with expressively wide eyes, and equally expressive shaking of the head. That any one should journey from Calabria to England seemed to him intelligible enough; but he marvelled that I had thought it worth while to come from England to Calabria. Very rarely indeed could he show his garden to one from a far-off country; no, the place was too poor, accommodation too rough; there needed a certain courage, and he laughed, again shaking his head.

The ordinary graves were marked with a small wooden cross; where a head-stone had been raised, it generally presented a skull and crossed bones. Round the enclosure stood a number of mortuary chapels, gloomy and ugly. An exception to this dull magnificence in death was a marble slab, newly set against the wall, in memory of a Lucifero—one of that family, still eminent, to which belonged the sacrilegious bishop.[4] The design was a good imitation of those noble sepulchral tablets which abound in the museum at Athens[5]; a figure taking leave of others as if going on a journey. The Lucifers had shown good taste in their choice of the old Greek symbol; no better adornment of a tomb has ever been devised, nor one that is half so moving. At the foot of the slab was carved a little owl (civetta), a bird, my friend informed me, very common about here.

When I took leave, the kindly fellow gave me a large bunch of flowers, carefully culled, with many regrets that the lateness of the season forbade his offering choicer blossoms. His simple good-nature and intelligence greatly won upon me. I like to think of him as still quietly happy amid his garden walls, tending flowers that grow over the dead at Cotrone.[6]

On my way back again to the town, I took a nearer view of the ruined little church[7], and, whilst I was so engaged, two lads driving a herd of goats stopped to look at me. As I came out into the road again, the younger of these modestly approached and begged me to give him a flower—by choice, a rose. I did so, much to his satisfaction and no less to mine; it was a pleasant thing to find a wayside lad asking for anything but soldi. The Calabrians, however, are distinguished by their self-respect; they contrast remarkably with the natives of the Neapolitan district. Presently, I saw that the boy's elder companion had appropriated the flower, which he kept at his nose as he plodded along; after useless remonstrance, the other drew near to me again, shamefaced; would I make him another present; not a rose this time, he would not venture to ask it, but "*questo piccolo*"; and he pointed to a sprig of geranium. There was a grace about the little lad which led me to talk to him, though I found his dialect very difficult. Seeing us on good terms, the elder boy drew near, and at once asked a puzzling question: When was the ruined church on the hillside to be rebuilt? I answered, of course, that I knew nothing about it, but this reply was taken as merely evasive; in a minute or two the lad again questioned me. Was the rebuilding to be next year? Then I began to understand; having seen me examining the ruins, the boy took it for granted that I was an architect here on business, and I don't think I succeeded in setting him right. When he had said good-bye he turned to look after me with a mischievous smile, as much as to say that I had naturally refused to talk to him about so important a matter as the building of a church, but *he* was not to be deceived.

The common type of face at Cotrone is coarse and bumpkinish; ruder, it seemed to me, than faces seen at any point of my journey hitherto. A photographer had hung out a lot of portraits, and it was a hideous exhibition; some of the visages attained an incredible degree of vulgar ugliness. This in the town which still bears the name of Croton. The people are all more or less unhealthy; one meets peasants horribly disfigured with life-long malaria. There is an agreeable cordiality in the middle classes; business men from whom I sought casual information, even if we only exchanged a few words in the street, shook hands with me at parting. I found no one who had much good to say of his native place; every one complained of a lack of water. Indeed, Cotrone has as good as no water supply. One or two wells I saw, jealously guarded: the water they yield is not really fit for drinking, and people who can afford it purchase water which comes from a distance in earthenware jars. One of these jars I had found in my bedroom; its secure corking much puzzled me until I made inquiries. The river Esaro is all but useless for any purpose, and as no other stream flows in the neighbourhood, Cotrone's washerwomen take their work down to the beach; even during the gale I saw them washing there in pools which they had made to hold the sea water; now and then one of them ventured into the surf, wading with legs of limitless nudity and plunging linen as the waves broke about her.

It was unfortunate that I brought no letter of introduction to Cotrone; I should much have liked to visit one of the better houses. Well-to-do people live here, and I was told that, in fine weather, "at least half a dozen" private carriages might be seen making the fashionable drive on the Strada Regina Margherita. But it is not easy to imagine luxury or refinement in these dreary, close-packed streets. Judging from our table at the *Concordia*, the town is miserably provisioned; the dishes were poor and monotonous and infamously cooked. Almost the only palatable thing offered was an enormous radish. Such radishes I never saw: they were from six to eight inches long, and more than an inch thick, at the same time thoroughly crisp and sweet. The wine of the country had nothing to recommend it. It was very heady, and smacked of drugs rather than of grape juice.

But men must eat, and the *Concordia*, being the only restaurant, daily entertained several citizens, besides guests staying in the house. One of these visitants excited my curiosity; he was a middle-aged man of austere countenance; shabby in attire, but with the bearing of one accustomed to command. Arriving always at exactly the same moment, he seated himself in his accustomed place, drew his hat over his brows, and began to munch bread. No word did I hear him speak. As soon as he appeared in the doorway, the waiter called out, with respectful hurry, "Don Ferdinando!" and in a minute his first course was served. Bent like a hunchback over the table, his hat dropping ever lower, until it almost hid his eyes, the Don ate voraciously. His dishes seemed to be always the same, and as soon as he had finished the last mouthful, he rose and strode from the room.

Don is a common title of respect in Southern Italy; it dates of course from the time of Spanish rule. At a favourable moment I ventured to inquire of the waiter who Don Ferdinando might be; the only answer, given with extreme discretion, was "A proprietor". If in easy circumstances, the Don must have been miserly, his diet was wretched beyond description. And in the manner of his feeding he differed strangely from the ordinary Italian who frequents restaurants. Wonderful to observe, the representative diner. He always seems to know exactly what his appetite demands; he addresses the waiter in a preliminary discourse, sketching out his meal, and then proceeds to fill in the minutiae. If he orders a common dish, he describes with exquisite detail how it is to be prepared; in demanding something out of the way he glows with culinary enthusiasm. An ordinary bill of fare never satisfies him; he plays variations upon the theme suggested, divides or combines, introduces novelties of the most unexpected kind. As a rule, he eats enormously (I speak only of dinner), a piled dish of macaroni is but the prelude to his meal, a whetting of his appetite. Throughout he grumbles, nothing is quite as it should be, and when the bill is presented he grumbles still more vigorously, seldom paying the sum as it stands. He rarely appears content with his entertainment, and often indulges in unbounded abuse of those who serve him. These characteristics, which I have noted more or less in every part of Italy, were strongly illustrated at the *Concordia*. In general, they consist with a fundamental good humour, but at Cotrone the tone of the dining-room was decidedly morose. One man—he seemed to be a sort of clerk—came only to quarrel. I am convinced that he ordered things which he knew the people could not cook just for the sake of reviling their handiwork when it was presented. Therewith he spent incredibly small sums; after growling and remonstrating and eating for more than an hour, his bill would amount to seventy or eighty centesimi, wine included. Every day he threatened to withdraw his custom; every day he sent for the landlady, pointed out to her how vilely he was treated, and asked how she could expect him to recommend the *Concordia* to his acquaintances. On one occasion I saw him push away a plate of something, plant his elbows on the table, and hide his face in his hands; thus he sat for ten

Plaque commemorating François Lenormant, George Gissing, Norman Douglas and Dr. Riccardo Sculco at the entrance of the former Albergo Concordia

minutes, an image of indignant misery, and when at length his countenance was again visible, it showed traces of tears.

I dwell upon the question of food because it was on this day that I began to feel a loss of appetite and found myself disgusted with the dishes set before me. In ordinary health I have that happiest qualification of the traveller, an ability to eat and enjoy the familiar dishes of any quasi-civilized country; it was a bad sign when I grew fastidious. After a mere pretence of dinner, I lay down in my room to rest and read. But, I could do neither; it grew plain to me that I was feverish. Through a sleepless night, the fever manifestly increasing, I wished that illness had fallen on me anywhere rather than at Cotrone.

9
My Friend the Doctor

IN the morning I arose as usual, though with difficulty. I tried to persuade myself that I was merely suffering from a violent attack of dyspepsia, the natural result of *Concordia* diet. When the waiter brought my breakfast I regarded it with resentful eye, feeling for the moment very much like my grumbling acquaintance of the dinner hour. It may be as well to explain that the breakfast consisted of very bad coffee, with goat's milk, hard, coarse bread, and goat's butter, which tasted exactly like indifferent lard. The so-called butter, by a strange custom of Cotrone, was served in the emptied rind of half a spherical cheese—the small *cacio cavallo*, horse cheese, which one sees everywhere in the South.[1] I should not have liked to inquire where, how, when, or by whom the substance of the cheese had been consumed. Possibly this receptacle is supposed to communicate a subtle flavour to the butter; I only know that, even to a healthy palate, the stuff was rather horrible. Cow's milk could be obtained in very small quantities, but it was of evil flavour; butter, in the septentrional sense of the word, did not exist.

It surprises me to remember that I went out, walked down to the shore, and watched the great waves breaking over the harbour mole. There was a lull in the storm, but as yet no sign of improving weather; clouds drove swiftly across a lowering sky. My eyes turned to the Lacinian promontory, dark upon the turbid sea. Should I ever stand by the sacred column? It seemed to me hopelessly remote; the voyage an impossible effort.

I talked with a man, of whom I remember nothing but his piercing eyes steadily fixed upon me; he said there had been a wreck in the night, a ship carrying live pigs had gone to pieces, and the shore was sprinkled with porcine corpses.

Presently I found myself back at the *Concordia*, not knowing exactly how I had returned. The dyspepsia—I clung to this hypothesis—was growing so violent that I had difficulty in breathing: before long I found it impossible to stand. Clearly, I must send for a doctor.

My hostess was summoned, and she told me that Cotrone had "a great physician", by name "Dr. Scurco". Translating this name from dialect into Italian, I presumed that the physician's real name was Sculco, and this proved to be the case.[2] Dr. Riccardo Sculco was a youngish man, with an open, friendly countenance. At once I liked him. After an examination, of which I quite understood the result, he remarked in his amiable, airy manner that I had "a touch of rheumatism"; as a simple matter of precaution, I had better go to bed for the rest of the day, and, just for the form of the thing, he would send some medicine. Having listened to this with as pleasant a smile as I could command, I caught the Doctor's eye, and asked quietly, "Is there much congestion?" His manner at once changed; he became businesslike and confidential. The right lung; yes, the right lung. Mustn't worry; get to bed and take my quinine in *dosi forti*, and he would look in again at night.

The second visit I but dimly recollect. There was a colloquy between the Doctor and my hostess, and the word *cataplasma* sounded repeatedly; also I heard again "*dosi forti*." The night that followed was

Dr. Riccardo Sculco,
the Cotrone physician

perhaps the most horrible I ever passed. Crushed with a sense of uttermost fatigue, I could get no rest. From time to time a sort of doze crept upon me, and I said to myself, "Now I shall sleep"; but on the very edge of slumber, at the moment when I was falling into oblivion, a hand seemed to pluck me back into consciousness. In the same instant there gleamed before my eyes a little circle of fire, which blazed and expanded into immensity, until its many-coloured glare beat upon my brain and thrilled me with torture. No sooner was the intolerable light extinguished than I burst into a cold sweat; an icy river poured about me; I shook, and my teeth chattered, and so for some minutes I lay in anguish, until the heat of fever re-asserted itself, and I began once more to toss and roll. A score of times was this torment repeated. The sense of personal agency forbidding me to sleep grew so strong that I waited in angry dread for that shock which aroused me; I felt myself haunted by a malevolent power, and rebelled against its cruelty.

Through the night no one visited me. At eight in the morning a knock sounded at the door, and there entered the waiter, carrying a tray with my ordinary breakfast.[3] "The Signore is not well?" he remarked, standing to gaze at me. I replied that I was not quite well; would he give me the milk, and remove from my sight as quickly as possible all the other things on the tray. A glimpse of butter in its cheese-rind had given me an unpleasant sensation. The goat's milk I swallowed thankfully, and, glad of the daylight, lay somewhat more at my ease awaiting Dr. Sculco.

He arrived about half-past nine, and was agreeably surprised to find me no worse. But the way in which his directions had been carried out did not altogether please him. He called the landlady, and soundly rated her. This scene was interesting, it had a fine flavour of the Middle Ages. The Doctor addressed mine hostess of the *Concordia* as "thou", and with magnificent disdain refused to hear her excuses; she, the stout, noisy woman, who ruled her own underlings with contemptuous rigour, was all subservience before this social superior, and whined to him for pardon. "What water is this?" asked Dr. Sculco, sternly, taking up the corked jar that stood on the floor. The hostess replied that it was drinking water, purchased with good money. Thereupon he poured out a little, held it up to the light, and remarked in a matter-of-fact tone, "I don't believe you."

However, in a few minutes peace was restored, and the Doctor prescribed anew. After he had talked about quinine and cataplasms, he asked me whether I had any appetite. A vision of the dining-room came before me, and I shook my head. "Still," he urged, "it would be well to eat something." And, turning to the hostess, "He had better have a beefsteak and a glass of Marsala." The look of amazement with which I heard this caught the Doctor's eye. "Don't you like *bistecca*?" he inquired. I suggested that, for one in a very high fever, with a good deal of lung congestion, beefsteak seemed a trifle solid, and Marsala somewhat heating. "Oh!" cried he, "but we must keep the machine going." And thereupon he took his genial leave.

I had some fear that my hostess might visit upon me her resentment of the Doctor's reproaches; but nothing of the kind. When we were alone, she sat down by me, and asked what I should really like to eat. If I did not care for a beefsteak of veal, could I eat a beefsteak of mutton? It was not the first time that such a choice had been offered me, for, in the South, *bistecca* commonly means a slice of meat done on the grill or in the oven. Never have I sat down to a *bistecca* which was fit for man's consumption, and, of course, at the *Concordia* it would be rather worse than anywhere else. I persuaded the good woman to supply me with a little broth. Then I lay looking at the patch of cloudy sky which showed above the houses opposite, and wondering whether I should have a second fearsome night. I wondered, too, how long it would be before I could quit Cotrone. The delay here was particularly unfortunate, as my letters were addressed to Catanzaro, the next stopping-place, and among them I expected papers which would need prompt attention.[4] The thought of trying to get my correspondence forwarded to Cotrone was too disturbing; it would have involved an enormous amount of trouble, and I could not have felt the least assurance that things would arrive safely. So I worried through the hours of daylight, and worried still more when, at nightfall, the fever returned upon me as badly as ever.

Dr. Sculco had paid his evening visit, and the first horror of ineffectual drowsing had passed over me, when my door was flung violently open, and in rushed a man (plainly of the commercial species), hat on head and bag in hand. I perceived that the *diligenza* had just arrived, and that travellers were seizing upon their bedrooms. The invader, aware of his mistake, discharged a volley of apologies, and rushed out again. Five minutes later the door again banged open, and there entered a tall lad with an armful of newspapers; after regarding me curiously, he asked whether I wanted a paper. I took one with the hope of reading it next morning. Then he began conversation. I had the fever? Ah! everybody had fever at Cotrone. He himself would be laid up with it in a day or two. If I liked, he would look in with a paper each evening—till fever prevented him. When I accepted this suggestion, he smiled encouragingly, cried "*Speriamo!*" and clumped out of the room.

I had as little sleep as on the night before, but my suffering was mitigated in a very strange way. After I had put out the candle, I tormented myself for a long time with the thought that I should never see La Colonna. As soon as I could rise from bed, I must flee Cotrone, and think myself fortunate in escaping alive; but to turn my back on the Lacinian promontory, leaving the Cape unvisited, the ruin of the temple unseen, seemed to me a miserable necessity which I should lament as long as I lived. I felt as one involved in a moral disaster; working in spite of reason, my brain regarded the matter from many points of view, and found no shadow of solace. The sense that so short a distance separated me from the place I desired to see, added exasperation to my distress. Half-delirious, I at times seemed to be in a boat, tossing on wild waters, the Column visible afar, but only when I strained my eyes to discover it. In a description of the approach by land, I had read of a great precipice which had to be skirted, and this, too, haunted me with its terrors: I found myself toiling on a perilous road, which all at once crumbled into fearful depths just before me. A violent shivering fit roused me from this gloomy dreaming, and I soon after fell into a visionary state which, whilst it lasted, gave me such placid happiness as I have never known when in my perfect mind. Lying still and calm, and perfectly awake, I watched a succession of wonderful pictures. First of all I saw great vases, rich with ornament and figures; then sepulchral marbles, carved more exquisitely than the most beautiful I had ever known. The vision grew in extent, in multiplicity of detail; presently I was regarding scenes of ancient life—thronged streets, processions triumphal or religious, halls of feasting, fields of battle. What most impressed me at the time was the marvellously bright yet delicate colouring of everything I saw. I can give no idea in words of the pure radiance which shone from every object, which illumined every scene. More remarkable, when I thought of it next day, was the minute finish of these pictures, the definiteness of every point on which my eye fell. Things which I could not know, which my imagination, working in the service of the will, could never have bodied forth, were before me as in life itself. I consciously wondered at peculiarities of costume such as I had never read of; at features of architecture entirely new to me; at insignificant characteristics of that by-gone world, which by no possibility could have been gathered from books. I recall a succession of faces, the loveliest conceivable; and I remember, I feel to this moment the pang of regret with which I lost sight of each when it faded into darkness.

As an example of the more elaborate visions that passed before me, I will mention the only one which I clearly recollect. It was a glimpse of history. When Hannibal, at the end of the second Punic War, was confined to the south of Italy, he made Croton his head-quarters, and when in reluctant obedience to Carthage, he withdrew from Roman soil, it was at Croton that he embarked. He then had with him a contingent of Italian mercenaries, and, unwilling that these soldiers should go over to the enemy, he bade them accompany him to Africa. The Italians refused. Thereupon Hannibal had them led down to the shore of the sea, where he slaughtered one and all. This event I beheld.[5] I saw the strand by Croton; the promontory with its temple; not as I know the scene to-day, but as it must have looked to those eyes more than two thousand years ago. The soldiers of Hannibal doing massacre, the perishing mercenaries, supported my closest gaze, and left no curiosity unsatisfied. (Alas! could I but see it again, or remember clearly what was shown me!) And over all lay a glory of sunshine, an indescribable brilliancy which puts light and warmth into my mind whenever I try to recall it. The delight of these phantasms was well worth the ten days' illness which paid for them. After this night they never returned; I hoped for their renewal, but in vain. When I spoke of the experience to Dr. Sulco, he was much amused, and afterwards he often asked me whether I had had any more *visioni*. That gate of dreams was closed, but I shall always feel that, for an hour, it was granted me to see the vanished life so dear to my imagination. If the picture corresponded to nothing real, tell me who can, by what power I reconstructed, to the last perfection of intimacy, a world known to me only in ruined fragments.

Daylight again, but no gleam of sun. I longed for the sunshine; it seemed to me a miserable chance that I should lie ill by the Ionian Sea and behold no better sky than the far north might have shown me. That grey obstruction of heaven's light always weighs upon my spirit; on a summer day, there has but to pass a floating cloud, which for a moment veils the sun, and I am touched with chill discouragement; heart and hope fail me, until the golden radiance is restored.

About noon, when I had just laid down the newspaper bought the night before—the Roman *Tribuna*, which was full of dreary politics—a sudden clamour in the street drew my attention. I heard the angry shouting of many voices, not in the piazza before the hotel, but at some little distance; it was impossible to distinguish any meaning in the tumultuous cries. This went on for a long time, swelling at moments into a roar of frenzied rage, then sinking to an uneven growl, broken by spasmodic yells. On asking what it meant, I was told that a crowd of poor folk had gathered before the Municipio to demonstrate against an oppressive tax called the *fuocatico*. This is simply hearth-money, an impost on each fireplace where food is cooked; the same tax which made trouble in old England, and was happily got rid of long ago. But the hungry plebs of Cotrone lacked vigour for any effective self-assertion; they merely exhausted themselves with shouting *"Abbass' 'o sindaco!"* and dispersed to the hearths which paid for an all but imaginary service. I wondered whether the Sindaco and his portly friend sat in their comfortable room whilst the roaring went on; whether they smoked their cigars as usual, and continued to chat at their ease. Very likely. The privileged classes in Italy are slow to move, and may well believe in the boundless endurance of those below them. Some day, no doubt, they will have a disagreeable surprise. When Lombardy begins in earnest to shout *"Abbasso!"* it will be an uneasy moment for the heavy syndics of Calabria.

Agave • Agave

10
Children of the Soil

ANY northern person who passed a day or two at the *Concordia* as an ordinary traveller would carry away a strong impression. The people of the house would seem to him little short of savages, filthy, in person and in habits, utterly uncouth in their demeanour, perpetual wranglers and railers, lacking every qualification for the duties they pretended to discharge. In England their mere appearance would revolt decent folk. With my better opportunity of judging them, I overcame the first natural antipathy; I saw their good side, and learnt to forgive the faults natural to a state of frank barbarism. It took two or three days before their rough and ready behaviour softened to a really human friendliness, but this came about at last, and when it was known that I should not give much more trouble, that I needed only a little care in the matter of diet, goodwill did its best to aid hopeless incapacity.

Whilst my fever was high, little groups of people often came into the room, to stand and stare at me, exchanging, in a low voice, remarks which they supposed I did not hear, or, hearing, could not understand; as a matter of fact, their dialect was now intelligible enough to me, and I knew that they discussed my chances of surviving. Their natures were not sanguine. A result, doubtless, of the unhealthy climate, every one at Cotrone seemed in a more or less gloomy state of mind. The hostess went about uttering ceaseless moans and groans; when she was in my room I heard her constantly sighing, "Ah, Signore! Ah, Cristo!"— exclamations which, perhaps, had some reference to my illness, but which did not cease when I recovered. Whether she had any private reason for depression I could not learn; I fancy not; it was only the whimpering and querulous habit due to low health. A female servant[1], who occasionally brought me food (I found that she also cooked it), bore herself in much the same way. This domestic was the most primitive figure of the household. Picture a woman of middle age, wrapped at all times in dirty rags (not to be called clothing), obese, grimy, with dishevelled black hair, and hands so scarred, so deformed by labour and neglect, as to be scarcely human. She had the darkest and fiercest eyes I ever saw. Between her and her mistress went on an unceasing quarrel: they quarrelled in my room, in the corridor, and, as I knew by their shrill voices, in places remote; yet I am sure they did not dislike each other, and probably neither of them ever thought of parting. Unexpectedly, one evening, this woman entered, stood by the bedside, and began to talk with such fierce energy, with such flashing of her black eyes, and such distortion of her features, that I could only suppose that she was attacking me for the trouble I caused her. A minute or two passed before I could even hit the drift of her furious speech; she was always the most difficult of the natives to understand, and in rage she became quite unintelligible. Little by little, by dint of questioning, I got at what she meant. There had been *guai* [2], worse than usual; the mistress had reviled her unendurably for some fault or other, and was it not hard that she should be used like this after having *tanto, tanto lavorato!* In fact, she was appealing for my sympathy, not abusing me at all. When she went on to say that she was alone in the world, that all her kith and kin were *freddi morti* (stone dead), a pathos in her aspect and her words took hold upon me; it was much as if some heavy-laden beast of burden had suddenly found tongue, and protested in the rude beginnings of articulate utterance against its hard lot. If only one could have learnt, in intimate detail, the life of this domestic serf! How interesting, and how sordidly picturesque against the background of romantic landscape, of scenic history! I looked long into her sallow, wrinkled face, trying to imagine the thoughts that ruled its expression. In some measure my efforts at kindly speech succeeded, and her "Ah, Cristo!" as she turned to go away, was not without a touch of solace.

Another time my hostess fell foul of the waiter because he had brought me goat's milk which was very sour. There ensued the most comical scene. In an access of fury the stout woman raged and stormed; the waiter, a lank young fellow, with a simple, good-natured face, after trying to explain that he had committed the fault by inadvertence, suddenly raised his hand, like one about to exhort a congregation, and exclaimed in a tone of injured remonstrance, "*Un po' di calma! Un po' di calma!*" My explosion of laughter at this inimitable utterance put an end to the strife. The youth laughed with me; his mistress bustled him out of the room, and then began to inform me that he was weak in his head. Ah! she exclaimed, her life with these people! what it cost her to keep them in anything like order! When she retired, I heard her expectorating violently in the corridor; a habit with every inmate of this genial hostelry.

When the worst of my fever had subsided, the difficulty was to obtain any nourishment suitable to my state. The good doctor, who had suggested beefsteak and Marsala when I was incapable of taking anything at all, ruled me severely in the matter of diet now that I really began to feel hungry. I hope I may never again be obliged to drink goat's milk; in these days it became so unutterably loathsome to me that I had, at length, to give it up altogether, and I cannot think of it now without a qualm. The broth offered me was infamous, mere coloured water beneath half an inch of floating grease. Once there was promise of fowl, and I looked forward to it eagerly; but, alas! this miserable bird had undergone a process of seething for the extraction of soup. I would have defied any one to distinguish between the substance remaining and two or three old kid gloves boiled into a lump. With a pleased air, the hostess one day suggested a pigeon, a roasted pigeon, and I welcomed the idea joyously. Indeed, the appearance of the dish, when it was borne in, had nothing to discourage my appetite—the odour was savoury; I prepared myself for a treat. Out of pure kindness, for she saw me tremble in my weakness, the good woman offered her aid in the carving; she took hold of the bird by the two legs, rent it asunder, tore off the wings in the same way, and then, with a smile of satisfaction, wiped her hands upon her skirt. If her hands had known water (to say nothing of soap) during the past twelve months I am much mistaken. It was a pity, for I found that my teeth could just masticate a portion of the flesh which hunger compelled me to assail.

Of course I suffered much from thirst, and Dr. Sculco startled me one day by asking if I liked *tea*. Tea? Was it really procurable? The Doctor assured me that it could be supplied by the chemist; though, considering how rarely the exotic was demanded, it might have lost something of its finer flavour whilst stored at the pharmacy. An order was despatched. Presently the waiter brought me a very small paper packet, such as might have contained a couple of Seidlitz powders; on opening it I discovered something black and triturated, a crumbling substance rather like ground charcoal. I smelt it, but there was no perceptible odour; I put a little of it to my tongue, but the effect was merely that of dust. Proceeding to treat it as if it were veritable tea, I succeeded in imparting a yellowish tinge to the hot water, and, so thirsty was I, this beverage tempted me to a long draught. There followed no ill result that I know of, but the paper packet lay thenceforth untouched, and, on leaving, I made a present of it to my landlady.

To complete the domestic group, I must make mention of the "chambermaid". This was a lively little fellow of about twelve years old, son of the landlady, who gave me much amusement. I don't know whether he performed chambermaid duty in all the rooms; probably the fierce-eyed cook did the heavier work elsewhere, but upon me his attendance was constant. At an uncertain hour of the evening he entered (of course, without knocking), doffed his cap in salutation, and began by asking how I found myself. The question could not have been more deliberately and thoughtfully put by the Doctor himself. When I replied that I was better, the little man expressed his satisfaction, and went on to make a few remarks about the *pessimo tempo*. Finally, with a gesture of politeness, he inquired whether I would permit him "*di fare un po' di pulizia*"—to clean up a little, and this he proceeded to do with much briskness. Excepting the good Sculco, my chambermaid was altogether the most civilized person I met at Cotrone. He had a singular amiability of nature, and his boyish spirits were not yet subdued by the pestilent climate. If I thanked him for anything, he took off his cap, bowed with comical dignity, and answered "*Grazie a voi, Signore.*" Of course these people never used the third person feminine of polite Italian. Dr. Sculco did so, for I had begun by addressing him in that manner, but plainly it was not familiar to his lips. At the same time there prevailed certain forms of civility, which seemed a trifle excessive. For instance, when the Doctor entered my room, and I gave him "*Buon giorno,*" he was wont to reply, "*Troppo gentile!*"—too kind of you!

My newspaper boy came regularly for a few days, always complaining of feverish symptoms, then ceased to appear. I made inquiry: he was down with illness, and as no one took his place I suppose the regular distribution of newspapers in Cotrone was suspended. When the poor fellow again showed himself, he had a sorry visage; he sat down by my bedside (rain dripping from his hat, and mud, very thick, upon his boots) to give an account of his sufferings. I pictured the sort of retreat in which he had lain during those miserable hours. My own chamber contained merely the barest necessaries, and, as the gentleman of Cosenza would have said, "left something to be desired" in point of cleanliness. Conceive the places into which Cotrone's poorest have to crawl when they are stricken with disease. I admit, however, that the thought was worse to me at that moment than it is now. After all, the native of Cotrone has advantages over the native of a city slum; and it is better to die in a hovel by the Ionian Sea than in a cellar at Shoreditch.

The position of my room, which looked upon the piazza, enabled me to hear a great deal of what went on in the town. The life of Cotrone began about three in the morning; at that hour I heard the first voices, upon which there soon followed the bleating of goats and the tinkling of ox-bells. No doubt the greater part of the poor people were in bed by eight o'clock every evening; only those who had dealings in the outer world were stirring when the *diligenza* arrived about ten, and I suspect that some of these snatched a nap before that late hour. Throughout the day there sounded from the piazza a ceaseless clamour of voices, such a noise as in England would only rise from some excited crowd on a rare occasion; it was increased by reverberation from the colonnade which runs all round in front of the shops. When the north-east gale had passed over, there ensued a few days of sullen calm, permitting the people to lead their ordinary life in open air. I grew to recognize certain voices, those of men who seemingly had nothing to do but to talk all day long. Only the sound reached me; I wish I could have gathered the sense of these interminable harangues and dialogues. In every country and every age those talk most who have least to say that is worth saying. These tonguesters of Cotrone had their predecessors in the public place of Croton, who began to gossip before dawn, and gabbled unceasingly till after nightfall; with their voices must often have mingled the bleating of goats or the lowing of oxen, just as I heard the sounds to-day.

One day came a street organ, accompanied by singing, and how glad I was! The first note of music, this, that I had heard at Cotrone. The instrument played only two or three airs, and one of them became a great favourite with the populace; very soon, numerous voices joined with that of the singer, and all this and the following day the melody sounded, near or far. It had the true characteristics of southern song; rising tremolos, and cadences that swept upon a wail of passion; high falsetto notes, and deep tum-tum of infinite melancholy. Scorned by the musician, yet how expressive of a people's temper, how suggestive of its history! At the moment when this strain broke upon my ear, I was thinking ill of Cotrone and its inhabitants; in the first pause of the music I reproached myself bitterly for narrowness and ingratitude. All the faults of the Italian people are whelmed in forgiveness as soon as their music sounds under the Italian sky. One remembers all they have suffered, all they have achieved in spite of wrong. Brute races have flung themselves, one after another, upon this sweet and glorious land; conquest and slavery, from age to age, have been the people's lot. Tread where one will, the soil has been drenched with blood. An immemorial woe sounds even through the lilting notes of Italian gaiety. It is a country wearied and regretful, looking ever backward to the things of old; trivial in its latter life, and unable to hope sincerely for the future.

Moved by these voices singing over the dust of Croton, I asked pardon for all my foolish irritation, my impertinent fault-finding. Why had I come hither, if it was not that I loved land and people? And had I not richly known the recompense of my love?

Legitimately enough one may condemn the rulers of Italy, those who take upon themselves to shape her political life, and recklessly load her with burdens insupportable. But among the simple on Italian soil a wandering stranger has no right to nurse national superiorities, to indulge a contemptuous impatience. It is the touch of tourist vulgarity. Listen to a Calabrian peasant singing as he follows his oxen along the furrow, or as he shakes the branches of his olive tree. That wailing voice amid the ancient silence, that long lament solacing ill-rewarded toil, comes from the heart of Italy herself, and wakes the memory of mankind.

11
The Mount of Refuge

MY thoughts turned continually to Catanzaro. It is a city set upon a hill, overlooking the Gulf of Squillace, and I felt that if I could but escape thither, I should regain health and strength. Here at Cotrone the air oppressed and enfeebled me; the neighbourhood of the sea brought no freshness. From time to time the fever seemed to be overcome, but it lingered still in my blood and made my nights restless. I must away to Catanzaro.

When first I spoke of this purpose to Dr. Sculco, he indulged my fancy, saying "Presently, presently!" A few days later, when I seriously asked him how soon I might with safety travel, his face expressed misgiving. Why go to Catanzaro? It was on the top of a mountain, and had a most severe climate; the winds at this season were terrible. In conscience he could not advise me to take such a step: the results might be very grave after my lung trouble. Far better wait at Cotrone for a week or two longer, and then go to Reggio, crossing perhaps to Sicily to complete my cure. The more Dr. Sculco talked of windy altitudes, the stronger grew my desire for such a change of climate, and the more intolerable seemed my state of languishment. The weather was again stormy, but this time blew sirocco; I felt its evil breath waste my muscles, clog my veins, set all my nerves a-tremble. If I stayed here much longer, I should never get away at all. A superstitious fear crept upon me; I remembered that my last visit had been to the cemetery.

One thing was certain: I should never see the column of Hera's temple. I made my lament on this subject to Dr. Sculco, and he did his best to describe to me the scenery of the Cape. Certain white spots which I had discovered at the end of the promontory were little villas, occupied in summer by the well-to-do citizens of Cotrone; the Doctor himself owned one, which had belonged to his father before him. Some of the earliest memories of his boyhood were connected with the Cape; when he had lessons to learn by heart, he often used to recite them walking round and round the great column. In the garden of his villa he at times amused himself with digging, and a very few turns of the spade sufficed to throw out some relic of antiquity. Certain Americans, he said, obtained permission not long ago from the proprietor of the ground on which the temple stood to make serious excavations, but as soon as the Italians heard of it, they claimed the site as a national monument; the work was forbidden, and the soil had to be returned to its former state. Hard by the ancient sanctuary is a chapel, consecrated to the Madonna del Capo; thither the people of Cotrone make pilgrimages, and hold upon the Cape a rude festival, which often ends in orgiastic riot.

All the surface of the promontory is bare; not a tree, not a bush, save for a little wooded hollow called Fossa del Lupo—the wolf's den. There, says legend, armed folk of Cotrone used to lie in wait to attack the corsairs who occasionally landed for water.

When I led him to talk of Cotrone and its people, the Doctor could but confirm my observations. He contrasted the present with the past; this fever-stricken and waterless village with the great city which was called the healthiest in the world. In his opinion the physical change had resulted from the destruction of forests, which brought with it a diminution of the rainfall. "At Cotrone," he said, "we have practically no rain. A shower now and then, but never a wholesome downpour." He had no doubt that, in ancient times, all the hills of the coast were wooded, as Sila still is, and all the rivers abundantly supplied with water. To-day there was scarce a healthy man in Cotrone: no one had strength to resist a serious illness. This state of things he took very philosophically; I noticed once more the frankly mediæval spirit in which he regarded the populace. Talking on, he interested me by enlarging upon the difference between southern Italians and those of the north. Beyond Rome a Calabrian never cared to go; he found himself in a foreign country, where his tongue betrayed him, and where his manners were too noticeably at variance with those prevailing. Italian unity, I am sure, meant little to the good Doctor, and appealed but coldly to his imagination.

I declared to him at length that I could endure no longer this dreary life of the sick-room; I must get into the open air, and, if no harm came of the experiment, I should leave for Catanzaro. "I cannot prevent you," was the Doctor's reply, but I am obliged to point out that you act on your own responsibility. It is *pericoloso*, it is *pericolosissimo!*[1] The terrible climate of the mountains!" However, I won his permission to leave the house, and acted upon it that same afternoon. Shaking and palpitating, I slowly descended the stairs to the colonnade; then, with a step like that of an old, old man, tottered across the piazza, my object being to reach the chemist's shop, where I wished to pay for the drugs that I had had and for the tea. When I entered, sweat was streaming from my forehead; I dropped into a chair, and for a minute or two could do nothing but recover nerve and breath. Never in my life had I suffered such a wretched sense of feebleness. The pharmacist looked at me with a gravely compassionate eye; when I told him I was the Englishman who had been ill, and that I wanted to leave to-morrow for Catanzaro, his compassion indulged itself more freely, and I could see quite well that he thought my plan of travel visionary. True, he said, the climate of Cotrone was trying to a stranger. He understood my desire to get away; but—Catanzaro! Was I aware that at Catanzaro I should suddenly find myself in a season of most rigorous winter? And the winds! One needed to be very strong even to stand on one's feet at Catanzaro. For all this I returned thanks, and, having paid my bill, tottered back to the *Concordia*. It seemed to be more than doubtful whether I should start on the morrow.

That evening I tried to dine. Don Ferdinando entered as usual, and sat mute through his unchanging meal; the grumbler grumbled and ate, as perchance he does to this day. I forced myself to believe that the food had a savour for me, and that the wine did not taste of drugs. As I sat over my pretended meal, I heard the sirocco moaning without, and at times a splash of rain against the window. Near me, two military men were exchanging severe comments on Calabria and its people. "*Che paese!* "—"What a country!" exclaimed one of them finally in disgust. Of course they came from the north, and I thought that their conversation was not likely to knit closer the bond between the extremes of Italy.

To my delight I looked forth next morning on a sunny and calm sky, such as I had not seen during all my stay at Cotrone. I felt better, and decided to leave for Catanzaro by train in the early afternoon. Shaking still, but heartened by the sunshine, I took a short walk, and looked for the last time at the Lacinian promontory. On my way back I passed a little building from which sounded an astonishing noise, a confused babel of shrill voices, blending now and then with a deep stentorian shout. It was the communal school—not during play-time, or in a state of revolt, but evidently engaged as usual upon its studies. The school-house was small, but the volume of clamour that issued from it would have done credit to two or three hundred children in unrestrained uproariousness. Curiosity held me listening for ten minutes; the tumult underwent no change of character, nor suffered the least abatement; the mature voice occasionally heard above it struck a cheery note, by no means one of impatience or stern command. Had I been physically capable of any effort, I should have tried to view that educational scene. The incident did me good, and I went on in a happier humour.

Which was not perturbed by something that fell under my eye soon afterwards. At a shop door hung certain printed cards, bearing a notice that "wood hay-makers", "wood binders", and "wood mowers" were "sold here". Not in Italian this, but in plain, blunt English; and to each announcement was added the name of an English manufacturing firm, with an agency at Naples. I have often heard the remark that Englishmen of business are at a disadvantage in their export trade because they pay no heed to the special requirements of foreign countries; but such a delightful illustration of their ineptitude had never come under my notice. Doubtless these alluring advertisements are widely scattered through agricultural Calabria. Who knows? they may serve as an introduction to the study of the English tongue.

Not without cordiality was my leave-taking. The hostess confided to me that, in the first days of my illness, she had felt sure I should die. Everybody had thought so, she added gaily; even Dr. Sculco had shaken his head and shrugged his shoulders; much better, was it not, to be paying my bill? Bill more moderate, under the circumstances, no man ever discharged; Calabrian honesty came well out of the transaction.[2] So I tumbled once more into the dirty, ramshackle *diligenza*, passed along the dusty road between the barred and padlocked warehouses, and arrived in good time at the station. No sooner had I set foot on the platform than I felt an immense relief. Even here, it seemed to me, the air was fresher. I lifted my eyes to the hills and seemed to feel the breezes of Catanzaro.

The train was made up at Cotrone, and no undue haste appeared in our departure. When we were already twenty minutes late, there stepped into the carriage where I was sitting a good-humoured railway official, who smiled and greeted me. I supposed he wanted my ticket, but nothing of the kind. After looking all round the compartment with an air of disinterested curiosity, he heaved a sigh and remarked pleasantly to me, "*Non manca niente*"—"Nothing is amiss." Five minutes more and we steamed away.

The railway ascended a long valley, that of the Esaro, where along the deep watercourse trickled a scarce perceptible stream. On either hand were hills of pleasant outline, tilled on the lower slopes, and often set with olives. Here and there came a grassy slope, where shepherds or goatherds idled amid their flocks. Above the ascent a long tunnel, after which the line falls again towards the sea. The landscape took a nobler beauty; mountains spread before us, tenderly coloured by the autumn sun. We crossed two or three rivers—rivers of flowing water, their banks overhung with dense green jungle. The sea was azure, and looked very calm, but white waves broke loudly upon the strand, last murmur of the storm which had raged and renewed itself for nearly a fortnight.

At one of the wayside stations entered a traveller whom I could not but regard with astonishment. He was a man at once plump and muscular, his sturdy limbs well exhibited in a shooting costume. On his face glowed the richest hue of health; his eyes glistened merrily. With him he carried a basket, which, as soon as he was settled, gave forth an abundant meal. The gusto of his eating, the satisfaction with which he eyed his glasses of red wine, excited my appetite. But who *was* he? Not, I could see, a tourist; yet how account for this health and vigour in a native of the district? I had not seen such a man since I set out upon my travels; the contrast he made with the figures of late familiar to me was so startling that I had much ado to avoid continuously gazing at him. His proximity did me good; the man radiated health.

When next the train stopped he exchanged words with some one on the platform, and I heard that he was going to Catanzaro. At once I understood. This jovial, ruddy-cheeked personage was a man of the hills. At Catanzaro I should see others like him; perhaps he fairly represented its inhabitants. If so, I had reason for my suspicion that poor fever-stricken Cotrone regarded with a sort of jealousy the breezy health of Catanzaro, which at the same time is a much more prosperous place. Later, I found that there did exist some acerbity of mutual criticism between the two towns, reminding one of civic rivalry among the Greeks. Catanzaro spoke with contempt of Cotrone. Happily I made no medical acquaintance in the hill town; but I should have liked to discuss with one of these gentlemen the view of their climate held by Dr. Sculco.

In the ages that followed upon the fall of Rome, perpetual danger drove the sea-coast population of Calabria inland and to the heights. Our own day beholds a counter movement; the shore line of railway will create new towns on the old deserted sites. Such a settlement is the Marina of Catanzaro, a little port at the mouth of a wide valley, along which runs a line to Catanzaro itself, or rather to the foot of the great hill on which the town is situated. The sun was setting when I alighted at the Marina, and as I waited for the branch train my eyes feasted upon a glory of colour which made me forget aching weariness. All around lay orchards of orange trees, the finest I had ever seen, and over their solid masses of dark foliage, thick hung with ripening fruit, poured the splendour of the western sky. It was a picture unsurpassable in richness of tone; the dense leafage of deepest, warmest green glowed and flashed, its magnificence heightened by the blaze of the countless golden spheres adorning it. Beyond, the magic sea, purple and crimson as the sun descended upon the vanishing horizon. Eastward, above the slopes of Sila, stood a moon almost at its full, the yellow of an autumn leaf, on a sky soft-flushed with rose.

In my geography it is written that between Catanzaro and the sea lie the gardens of the Hesperides.

12
Catanzaro

FOR half an hour the train slowly ascends. The carriages are of special construction, light and many-windowed, so that one has good views of the landscape. Very beautiful was this long, broad, climbing valley, everywhere richly wooded; oranges and olives, carob and lentisk and myrtle, interspersed with cactus (its fruit, the prickly fig, all gathered) and with the sword-like agave. Glow of sunset lingered upon the hills; in the green hollow a golden twilight faded to dusk. The valley narrowed; it became a gorge between dark slopes which closed together and seemed to bar advance. Here the train stopped, and all the passengers (some half-dozen) alighted.

The sky was still clear enough to show the broad features of the scene before me. I looked up to a mountain side, so steep that towards the summit it appeared precipitous, and there upon the height, dimly illumined with a last reflex of after-glow, my eyes distinguished something which might be the outline of walls and houses. This, I knew, was the situation of Catanzaro, but one could not easily imagine by what sort of approach the city would be gained; in the thickening twilight, no trace of a road was discernible, and the flanks of the mountain, a ravine yawning on either hand, looked even more abrupt than the ascent immediately before me.

There, however, stood the *diligenza* which was somehow to convey me to Catanzaro; I watched its loading with luggage—merchandise and mailbags—whilst the exquisite evening melted into night. When I had thus been occupied for a few minutes, my look once more turned to the mountain, where a surprise awaited me: the summit was now encircled with little points of radiance, as though a starry diadem had fallen upon it from the sky. "*Pronti!*"[1] cried our driver. I climbed to my seat, and we began our journey towards the crowning lights.

General view with the highest bridge in Europe

By help of long loops the road ascended at a tolerably easy angle; the horse-bells tinkled, the driver shouted encouragement to his beasts, and within the vehicle went on a lively gossiping, with much laughter. Meanwhile the great moon had risen high enough to illumine the valley below us; silvery grey and green, the lovely hollow seemed of immeasurable length, and beyond it one imagined, rather than discerned, a glimmer of the sea. By the wayside I now and then caught sight of a huge cactus, trailing its heavy knotted length upon the face of a rock; and at times we brushed beneath overhanging branches of some tree that could not be distinguished. All the way up we seemed to skirt a sheer precipice, which at moments was alarming in its gloomy depth. Deeper and deeper below shone the lights of the railway station and of the few houses about it; it seemed as though a false step would drop us down into their midst.

The fatigue of the day's journey passed away during this ascent, which lasted nearly an hour; when, after a drive through dark but wide streets, I was set down before the hotel[2], I felt that I had shaken off the last traces of my illness. A keen appetite sent me as soon as possible in search of the dining-room, where I ate with extreme gusto; everything seemed excellent after the sorry table of the *Concordia*. I poured my wine with a free hand, rejoicing to find it was wine once more, and not (at all events to my palate) a concoction of drugs. The albergo was decent and well found; a cheerful prosperity declared itself in all I had yet seen. After dinner I stepped out on to the balcony of my room to view the city's main street; but there was very scant illumination, and the moonlight only showed me high houses of modern build. Few people passed, and never a vehicle; the shops were all closed. I needed no invitation to

The five-storey Albergo Centrale, c. 1905

sleep, but this shadowed stillness, and the fresh mountain air, happily lulled my thoughts. Even the subject of earthquakes proved soporific.

Impossible to find oneself at Catanzaro without thinking of earthquakes; I wonder that the good people of Cotrone did not include this among deterrents whereby they sought to prejudice me against the mountain town. Over and over again Catanzaro has been shaken to its foundations. The worst calamity recorded was towards the end of the eighteenth century[3], when scarce a house remained standing, and many thousands of the people perished. This explains a peculiarity in the aspect of the place, noticeable as soon as one begins to walk about; it is like a town either half built or half destroyed, one knows not which; everywhere one comes upon ragged walls, tottering houses, yet there is no appearance of antiquity. One ancient building, a castle built by Robert Guiscard when he captured Catanzaro in the eleventh century[4], remained until of late years, its Norman solidity defying earthquakes; but this has been pulled down, deliberately got rid of for the sake of widening a road. Lament over such a proceeding would be idle enough; Catanzaro is the one progressive town of Calabria, and has learnt too thoroughly the spirit of the time to suffer a blocking of its highway by middle-age obstructions.

If a Hellenic or Roman city occupied this breezy summit, it has left no name, and no relics of the old civilization have been discovered here. Catanzaro was founded in the tenth century, at the same time that Taranto was rebuilt after the Saracen destruction; an epoch of revival for Southern Italy under the vigorous Byzantine rule of Nicephorus Phocas.[5] From my point of view, the interest of the place suffered because I could attach to it no classic memory. Robert Guiscard, to be sure, is a figure picturesque enough, and might give play to the imagination, but I care little for him after all; he does not belong to my world. I had to see Catanzaro merely as an Italian town amid wonderful surroundings. The natural beauty of the spot amply sufficed to me during the days I spent there, and gratitude for health recovered gave me a kindly feeling to all its inhabitants.

Daylight brought no disillusion as regards natural features. I made the circuit of the little town, and found that it everywhere overlooks a steep, often a sheer, descent, save at one point, where an isthmus unites it to the mountains that rise behind. In places the bounding wall runs on the very edge of a precipice, and many a crazy house, overhanging, seems ready to topple into the abyss. The views are magnificent, whether one looks down the valley to the leafy shore, or, in an opposite direction, up to the grand heights which, at this narrowest point of Calabria, separate the Ionian from the Tyrrhene Sea. I could now survey the ravines which, in twilight, had dimly shown themselves on either side of the mountain; they are deep and narrow, craggy, wild, bare. Each, when the snows are melting, becomes the bed of a furious torrent; the watercourses uniting below to form the river of the valley. At this season there was a mere trickling of water over a dry brown waste. Where the abruptness of the descent does not render it impossible, olives have been planted on the mountain sides; the cactus clings everywhere, making picturesque many a wall and hovel, luxuriating on the hard, dry soil; fig trees and vines occupy more favoured spots, and the gardens of the better houses are often graced by a noble palm.

After my morning's walk I sought the residence of Signor Pasquale Cricelli, to whom I carried a note of introduction.[6] This gentleman holds the position of English Vice-Consul at Catanzaro, but it is seldom that he has the opportunity of conversing with English travellers; the courtesy and kindness with which he received me have a great part in my pleasant memory of the mountain town. Signor Cricelli took me to see many interesting things, and brought me into touch with the every-day life of Catanzaro. I knew from Lenormant's book that the town had a singular reputation for hospitality.[7] The French archæologist tells amusing stories in illustration of this characteristic. Once, when he had taken casual refreshment at a restaurant, a gentleman sitting at another table came forward and, with

Pasquale Cricelli
(1863-1905)

grave politeness, begged permission to pay for what Lenormant had consumed. This was a trifle in comparison with what happened when the traveller, desirous of making some return for much kindness, entertained certain of his acquaintances at dinner, the meal, naturally, as good a one as his hotel could provide. The festival went off joyously, but, to Lenormant's surprise, nothing was charged for it in his bill. On making inquiry he learnt that the cost of the entertainment had already been discharged by one of his guests! Well, that took place years ago, long before a railway had been thought of in the valley of the Corace; such heroic virtues ill consist with the life of to-day. Nevertheless, Don Pasquale (Signor Cricelli's name when greeted by his fellow-citizens) several times reminded me, without knowing it, of what I had read. For instance, we entered a shop which he thought might interest me; the salesman during our talk unobtrusively made up a little parcel of goods, and asked, at length, whether I would take this with me or have it sent to the hotel. That point I easily decided, but by no persistence could I succeed in paying for the things. Smiling behind his counter, the shopkeeper declined to name a price; Don Pasquale declared that payment under such circumstances was a thing unknown in Catanzaro, and I saw that to say anything more would be to run the risk of offending him. The same day he invited me to dinner, and explained that we must needs dine at the hotel where I was staying, this being the best place of entertainment in the town. I found that my friend had a second reason for the choice; he wished to ascertain whether I was comfortably lodged, and as a result of his friendly offices, various little changes came about. Once more I make my grateful acknowledgments to the excellent Don Pasquale.

Speaking of shops, I must describe in detail the wonderful pharmacy.[8] Signor Cricelli held it among the sights of Catanzaro; this chemist's in the main street was one of the first places to which he guided me. And, indeed, the interior came as a surprise. Imagine a spacious shop, well proportioned; perfectly contrived, and throughout fitted with woodwork copied from the best examples of old Italian carving. Seeking pill or potion, one finds oneself in a museum of art, where it would be easy to spend an hour in studying the counter, the shelves, the ceiling. The chemists (two brothers if I remember rightly)

Interior of the Farmacia Leone (1897)

pointed out to me with legitimate pride all that they had done for the beautifying of their place of business; I shall not easily forget the glowing countenance, the moved voice, which betrayed their feelings as they led me hither and thither; for them and their enterprise I felt a hearty respect. When we had surveyed everything within doors I

Part of the counter still to be seen in the former Farmacia Leone

was asked to look at the *mostra*—the sign that hung over the entrance; a sort of griffin in wrought iron, this, too, copied from an old masterpiece, and reminding one of the fine ironwork which adorns the streets of Siena.[9] Don Pasquale could not be satisfied until I had privately assured him of my genuine admiration. Was it, he asked, at all like a chemist's shop in London? My reply certainly gratified him, but I am afraid it did not increase his desire to visit England.

Whilst I was at the chemist's, there entered a number of peasants, whose appearance was so striking that I sought information about them. Don Pasquale called them "*Greci*"; they came from a mountain village where the dialect of the people is still a corrupt Greek. One would like to imagine that their origin dates back to the early Hellenic days, but it is assuredly much later. These villages may be a relic of the Byzantine conquest in the sixth century, when Southern Italy was, to a great extent, re-peopled from the Eastern Empire, though another theory suggests that they were formed by immigrants from Greece at the time of the Turkish invasion.[10] Each of the women had a baby hanging at her back, together with miscellaneous goods which she had purchased in the town: though so heavily burdened, they walked erect, and with the free step of mountaineers.

I could not have had a better opportunity than was afforded me on this day of observing the peasantry of the Catanzaro district. It was the

The sign still hanging outside the former Farmacia Leone

feast of the Immaculate Conception, and from all around the country-folk thronged in pilgrimage to the church of the Immaculate; since earliest morning I had heard the note of bagpipes, which continued to sound before the street shrines all day long. Don Pasquale assured me that the festival had an importance in this region scarcely less than that of Christmas. At the hour of high mass I entered the sanctuary whither all were turning their steps; it was not easy to make a way beyond the portico, but when I had slowly pressed forward through the dense crowd, I found that the musical part of the service was being performed by a lively string-band, up in a gallery. For seats there was no room; a standing multitude filled the whole church before the altar, and the sound of gossiping voices at moments all but overcame that of the music. I know not at what point of the worship I chanced to be present; heat and intolerable odours soon drove me forth again, but I retained an impression of jollity, rather than of reverence. Those screaming and twanging instruments sounded much like an invitation to the dance, and all the faces about me were radiant with cheerfulness. Just such a throng, of course, attended upon the festival of god or goddess ere the old religion was transformed. Most of the Christian anniversaries have their origin in heathendom; the names have changed, but amid the unlettered worshippers there is little change of spirit; a tradition older than they can conceive rules their piety, and gives it whatever significance it may have in their simple lives.

Many came from a great distance; at the entrance to the town were tethered innumerable mules and asses, awaiting the hour of return. Modern Catanzaro, which long ago lost its proper costume, was enlivened with brilliant colours; the country women, of course, adorned themselves, and their garb was that which had so much interested me when I first saw it in the public garden at Cosenza. Brilliant blue and scarlet were the prevailing tones; a good deal of fine embroidery caught the eye. In a few instances I noticed men wearing the true Calabrian hat—peaked, brigandesque—which is rapidly falling out of use. These people were, in general, good-looking; frequently I observed a very handsome face, and occasionally a countenance, male or female, of really heroic beauty. Though crowds wandered through the streets, there sounded no tumult; voices never rose above an ordinary pitch of conversation; the general bearing was dignified, and tended to gravity. One woman in particular held my attention, not because of any exceptional beauty, for, indeed, she had a hard, stern face, but owing to her demeanour. Unlike most of the peasant folk, she was bent on business; carrying upon her head a heavy pile of some ornamented fabric—shawls or something of the kind—she entered shops, and paused at house doors, in the endeavour to find purchasers. I watched her for a long time, hoping she might make a sale, but ever she was unsuccessful; for all that she bore herself with a dignity not easily surpassed. Each offer of her wares was made as if she conferred a graceful favour, and after each rejection she withdrew unabashed, outwardly unperturbed, seeming to take stately leave. Only her persistence showed how anxious she was to earn money; neither on her features nor in her voice appeared the least sign of peddling solicitude. I shall always remember that tall, hard-visaged woman, as she passed with firm step and nobly balanced figure about the streets of Catanzaro. To pity her would have been an insult. The glimpse I caught of her laborious life revealed to me something worthy of admiration; never had I seen a harassing form of discouragement so silently and strongly borne.

13
The Breezy Height [1]

CATANZARO must be one of the healthiest spots in Southern Italy; perhaps it has no rival in this respect among the towns south of Rome. The furious winds, with which my acquaintances threatened me, did not blow during my stay, but there was always more or less breeze, and the kind of breeze that refreshes. I should like to visit Catanzaro in the summer; probably one would have all the joys of glorious sunshine without oppressive heat, and the landscape in those glowing days would be indescribably beautiful.

I remember with delight the public garden at Cosenza, its noble view over the valley of the Crati to the heights of Sila; that of Catanzaro is in itself more striking, and the prospect it affords has a sterner, grander note. Here you wander amid groups of magnificent trees, an astonishingly rich and varied vegetation; and from a skirting terrace you look down upon the precipitous gorge, burnt into barrenness save where a cactus clings to some jutting rock. Here in summer-time would be freshness amid noontide heat, with wondrous avenues of golden light breaking the dusk beneath the boughs. I shall never see it; but the desire often comes to me under northern skies, when I am weary of labour and seek in fancy a paradise of idleness.

In the public gardens is a little museum, noticeable mostly for a fine collection of ancient coins.[2] There are Greek pots, too, and weapons, found at Tiriolo, a village high up on the mountain above Catanzaro. As

The Villa Trieste, now the Villa Margherita

at Taranto, a stranger who cares for this kind of thing can be sure of having the museum all to himself. On my first visit Don Pasquale accompanied me, and through him I made the acquaintance of the custodian. But I was not in the museum mood; reviving health inclined me to the open air, and the life of to-day; I saw these musty relics with only a vague eye.

After living amid a malaria-stricken population, I rejoiced in the healthy aspect of the mountain folk. Even a deformed beggar, who dragged himself painfully along the pavement, had so ruddy a face that it was hard to feel compassion for him. And the wayside children—it was a pleasure to watch them at their games. Such children in Italy do not, as a rule, seem happy; too often they look ill, cheerless, burdened before their time; at Catanzaro they are as robust and lively as heart could wish, and their voices ring delightfully upon the ear. It is not only, I imagine, a result of the fine air they breathe; no doubt they are exceptional among the poor children of the South in getting enough to eat. The town has certain industries, especially the manufacture of silk; one feels an atmosphere of well-being; mendicancy is a rare thing.

Fruits abounded, and were very cheap; if one purchased from a stall the difficulty was to carry away the abundance offered for one's smallest coin. Excellent oranges cost about a penny the half-dozen. Any one who is fond of the prickly fig should go to Catanzaro. I asked a man sitting with a basket of them at a street corner to give me the worth of a soldo (a halfpenny); he began to fill my pocket, and when I cried that it was enough, that I could carry no more, he held up one particularly fine fruit, smiled as only an Italian can, and said, with admirable politeness, "*Questo per complimento!*" I ought to have shaken hands with him.

Even when I had grown accustomed to the place, its singular appearance of incompleteness kept exciting my attention. I had never seen a town so ragged at the edges. If there had recently been a great conflagration and almost all the whole city were being rebuilt, it would have looked much as it did at the time of my visit. To enter the post-office one had to clamber over heaps of stone and plaster, to stride over tumbled beams and jump across great puddles, entering at last by shaky stairs a place which looked like the waiting-room of an unfinished railway station. The style of building is peculiar, and looks so temporary as to keep one constantly in mind of the threatening earthquake. Most of the edifices, large and small, public and private, are constructed of rubble set in cement, with an occasional big, rough-squared stone to give an appearance of solidity, and perhaps a few courses of bricks in the old Roman style. If the building is of importance, this work is hidden beneath stucco; otherwise it remains like the mere shell of a house, and is disfigured over all its surface with great holes left by the scaffolding. Religion supplies something of adornment; above many portals is a rudely painted Virgin and Child, often, plainly enough, the effort of a hand accustomed to any tool rather than that of the artist. On the dwellings of the very poor a great Cross is scrawled in whitewash. These rickety houses often exhibit another feature more picturesque and, to the earthly imagination, more consoling; on the balcony one sees a great gourd, some three feet long, so placed that its yellow plumpness may ripen in sun and air. It is a sign of plenty: the warm spot of colour against the rough masonry does good to eye and heart.

My hotel afforded me little amusement after the *Concordia* at Cotrone, yet it did not lack its characteristic features. I found, for instance, in my bedroom a printed notice, making appeal in remarkable terms to all who occupied the chamber. The proprietor—thus it ran— had learnt with extreme regret that certain travellers who slept under his roof were in the habit of taking their meals at other places of entertainment. This practice, he desired it to be known, not only hurt his personal feelings—*tocca il suo morale*— but did harm to the reputation of the establishment. Assuring all and sundry that he would do his utmost to maintain a high standard of culinary excellence, the proprietor ended by begging his honourable clients that they would bestow their kind favours on the restaurant of the house—*si onora pregare i suoi rispettabili clienti perchè vogliano benignarsi il ristorante*; and therewith signed himself—Coriolano Paparazzo.[3]

Plaque commemorating Gissing's stay at the Albergo Centrale, as well as its proprietor in 1897, Coriolano Paparazzo

For my own part I was not tempted to such a breach of decorum; the fare provided by Signor Paparazzo suited me well enough, and the wine of the country was so good that, it would have covered many defects of cookery. Of my fellow-guests in the spacious dining-room I can recall only two. They were military men of a certain age, grizzled officers, who walked rather stiffly and seated themselves with circumspection. Evidently old friends, they always dined at the same time, entering one a few minutes after the other; but by some freak of habit they took places at different tables, so that the conversation which they kept up all through the meal had to be carried on by an exchange of shouts. Nothing whatever prevented them from being near each other; the room never contained more than half a dozen persons; yet thus they sat, evening after evening, many yards apart, straining their voices to be mutually audible. Me they delighted; to the other guests, more familiar with them and their talk, they must have been a serious nuisance. But I should have liked to see the civilian who dared to manifest his disapproval of these fine old warriors.

They sat interminably, evidently having no idea how otherwise to pass the evening. In the matter of public amusements Catanzaro is not progressive; I only once saw an announcement of a theatrical performance, and it did not smack of modern enterprise. On the dining-room table one evening lay a little printed bill, which made known that a dramatic company was then in the town. Their entertainment consisted of two parts, the first entitled: "The Death of Agolante and the Madness of Count Orlando"; the second "A Delightful Comedy, the Devil's Castle with Pulcinella as the Timorous Soldier". In addition were promised "new duets and Neapolitan songs". The theatre would comfortably seat three hundred persons, and the performance would be given twice, at half-past eighteen and half-past twenty-one o'clock. It was unpardonable in me that I did not seek out the Teatro delle Varietà⁴; I might easily have been in my seat (with thirty, more likely than three hundred, other spectators) by half-past twenty-one. But the night was forbidding; a cold rain fell heavily. Moreover, just as I had thought that it was perhaps worth while to run the risk of another illness—one cannot see the Madness of Count Orlando every day—there came into the room a peddler laden with some fifty volumes of fiction and a fine assortment of combs and shirt-studs. The books tempted me; I looked them through. Most, of course, were translations from the vulgarest French *feuilletonistes*; the Italian reader of novels, whether in newspaper or volume, knows, as a rule, nothing but this imported rubbish. However, a real Italian work was discoverable, and, together with the unfriendly sky, it kept me at home. I am sorry now, as for many another omission on my wanderings, when lack of energy or a passing mood of dullness has caused me to miss what would be so pleasant in the retrospect.

I spent an hour one evening at the principal café, where a pianist of great pretensions and small achievement made rather painful music. Watching and listening to the company (all men, of course, though the Oriental system regarding women is not so strict at Catanzaro as elsewhere in the South), I could not but fall into a comparison of this scene with any similar gathering of middle-class English folk. The contrast was very greatly in favour of the Italians. One has had the same thought a hundred times in the same circumstances, but it is worth dwelling upon. Among these representative men, young and old, of Catanzaro, the tone of conversation was incomparably better than that which would rule in a cluster of English provincials met to enjoy their evening leisure. They did, in fact, converse—a word rarely applicable to English talk under such conditions; mere personal gossip was the exception; they exchanged genuine thoughts, reasoned lucidly on the surface of abstract subjects. I say on the surface; no remark that I heard could be called original or striking; but the choice of topics and the mode of viewing them was distinctly intellectual. Phrases often occurred such as have no equivalent on the lips of everyday people in our own country. For instance, a young fellow in no way distinguished from his companions, fell to talking about a leading townsman, and praised him for his *ingenio simpatico*, his *bella intelligenza*, with exclamations of approval from those who listened. No, it is not merely the difference between homely Anglo-Saxon and a language of classic origin; there is a radical distinction of thought. These people have an innate respect for things of the mind, which is wholly lacking to a typical Englishman. One need not dwell upon the point that their animation was supported by a tiny cup of coffee or a glass of lemonade; this is a matter of climate and racial constitution; but I noticed the entire absence of a certain kind of jocoseness which is so naturally associated with spirituous liquors; no talk could have been less offensive. From many a bar-parlour in English country towns I have gone away heavy with tedium and disgust; the café at Catanzaro seemed, in comparison, a place of assembly for wits and philosophers.[5]

Meanwhile a season of rain had begun; heavy skies warned me that I must not hope for a renewal of sunny idleness on this mountain top; it would be well if intervals of cheerful weather lighted my further course by the Ionian Sea. Reluctantly, I made ready to depart.

14
Squillace

IN meditating my southern ramble I had lingered on the thought that I should see Squillace. For Squillace (Virgil's "ship-wrecking Scylaceum"[1]) was the ancestral home of Cassiodorus[2], and his retreat when he became a monk; Cassiodorus, the delightful pedant, the liberal statesman and patriot, who stands upon the far limit of his old Roman world and bids a sad farewell to its glories. He had niched himself in my imagination. Once when I was spending a silent winter upon the shore of Devon, I had with me the two folio volumes of his works, and patiently read the better part of them[3]; it was more fruitful than a study of all the modern historians who have written about his time. I saw the man; caught many a glimpse of his mind and heart, and names which had been to me but symbols in a period of obscure history became things living and recognizable.

I could have travelled from Catanzaro by railway to the sea-coast station called Squillace, but the town itself is perched upon a mountain some miles inland, and it was simpler to perform the whole journey by road, a drive of four hours, which, if the weather favoured me, would be thoroughly enjoyable. On my last evening Don Pasquale gave a good account of the sky; he thought I might hopefully set forth on the

View of the New Town from the road to the Ionian Sea

morrow, and, though I was to leave at eight o'clock, promised to come and see me off. Very early I looked forth, and the prospect seemed doubtful; I had half a mind to postpone departure. But about seven came Don Pasquale's servant, sent by his master to inquire whether I should start or not, and, after asking the man's opinion, I decided to take courage. The sun rose; I saw the streets of Catanzaro brighten in its pale gleams, and the rack above interspaced with blue.

Luckily my carriage-owner was a man of prudence; at the appointed hour he sent a covered vehicle—not the open *carrozzella* in which I should have cheerfully set forth had it depended upon myself. Don

Pasquale, too, though unwilling to perturb me, could not altogether disguise his misgivings. At my last sight of him, he stood on the pavement before the hotel gazing anxiously upwards. But the sun still shone, and as we began the descent of the mountain-side I felt annoyed at having to view the landscape through loopholes.

Of a sudden—we were near the little station down in the valley— there arose a mighty roaring, and all the trees of the wayside bent as if they would break. The sky blackened, the wind howled, and presently, as I peered through the window for some hope that this would only be a passing storm, rain beat violently upon my face. Then the carriage stopped, and my driver, a lad of about seventeen, jumped down to put something right in the horses' harness.

"Is this going to last?" I shouted to him.

"No, no, signore!" he answered gaily. "It will be over in a minute or two. *Ecco il sole!*"

I beheld no sun, either then or at any moment during the rest of the day, but the voice was so reassuring that I gladly gave ear to it. On we drove, down the lovely vale of the Corace, through orange-groves and pine-woods, laurels and myrtles, carobs and olive trees, with the rain beating fiercely upon us, the wind swaying all the leafage like billows on a stormy sea. At the Marina of Catanzaro we turned southward on the coast road, pursued it for two or three miles, then branched upon our inland way. The storm showed no sign of coming to an end. Several times the carriage stopped, and the lad got down to examine his horses—perhaps to sympathize with them; he was such a drenched, battered, pitiable object that I reproached myself for allowing him to pursue the journey.

"*Brutto tempo!*"[4] he screamed above the uproar, when I again spoke to him; but in such a cheery tone that I did not think it worth while to make any further remark.

Through the driving rain, I studied as well as I could the features of the country. On my left hand stretched a long flat-topped mountain, forming the southern slope of the valley we ascended; steep, dark, and furrowed with innumerable torrent-beds, it frowned upon a river that rushed along the ravine at its foot to pour into the sea where the mountain broke as a rugged cliff. This was the Mons Moscius[5] of old time, which sheltered the monastery built by Cassiodorus. The headlong, swollen flood, coloured like yellow clay, held little resemblance to the picture I had made of that river Pellena which murmurs so musically in the old writer's pages. Its valley was heaped with great blocks of granite—a feature which has interest for the geologist; it marks an abrupt change of system, from the soft stone of Catanzaro (which ends the Apennine) to that granitic mass of Aspromonte (the toe of Italy) which must have risen above the waters long before the Apennines came into existence. The wild weather emphasized a natural difference between this valley of Squillace and that which rises towards Catanzaro; here is but scanty vegetation, little more than thin orchards of olive, and the landscape has a bare, harsh character. Is it changed so greatly since the sixth century of our era? Or did its beauty lie in the eyes of Cassiodorus, who throughout his long life of statesmanship in the north never forgot this Bruttian home, and who sought peace at last amid the scenes of his childhood?

At windings of the way I frequently caught sight of Squillace itself, high and far, its white houses dull-gleaming against the lurid sky. The crag on which it stands is higher than that of Catanzaro, but of softer ascent. As we approached I sought for signs of a road that would lead us upward, but nothing of the sort could be discerned; presently I became aware that we were turning into a side valley, and, to all appearances, going quite away from the town. The explanation was that the ascent lay on the further slope; we began at length to climb the back of the mountain, and here I noticed with a revival of hope that there was a lull in the tempest; rain no longer fell so heavily; the clouds seemed to be breaking apart. A beam of sunshine would have set me singing with joy. When half-way up, my driver rested his horses and came to speak a word; we conversed merrily. He was to make straight for the hotel, where shelter and food awaited us—a bottle of wine, ha, ha! He knew the hotel, of course? Oh yes, he knew the hotel; it stood just at the entrance to the town; we should arrive in half an hour.

Looking upwards I saw nothing but a mass of ancient ruins, high fragments of shattered wall, a crumbling tower, and great windows through which the clouds were visible. Inhabited Squillace lay, no doubt, behind. I knew that it was a very small place, without any present importance; but at all events there was an albergo, and the mere name of albergo had a delightful sound of welcome after such a journey. Here I would stay for the night, at all events; if the weather cleared, I might be glad to remain for two or three days. Certainly the rain was stopping; the wind no longer howled. Up we went towards those ragged walls and great, vacant windows. We reached the summit; for two minutes the horses trotted; then a sudden halt, and my lad's face at the carriage door.

Ecco l'albergo, Signore!

I jumped out. We were at the entrance to an unpaved street of squalid hovels, a street which the rain had converted into a muddy river, so that, on quitting the vehicle, I stepped into running water up to my ankles. Before me was a long low cabin, with a row of four or five windows and no upper storey; a miserable hut of rubble and plaster, stained with ancient dirt and, at this moment, looking soaked with moisture. Above the doorway I read "Osteria Centrale"; on the bare end of the house was the prouder inscription, "Albergo Nazionale"—the National Hotel.[6] I am sorry to say that at the time this touch of humour made no appeal to me; my position was no laughing matter. Faint with hunger, I saw at once that I should have to browse on fearsome food. I saw, too, that there was scarce a possibility of passing the

The Albergo Nazionale, nowadays 37 via Damiano Assanti

night in this place; I must drive down to the sea-shore, and take my chance of a train which would bring me at some time to Reggio. While I thus reflected—the water rushing over my boots—a very ill-looking man came forth and began to stare curiously at me. I met his eye, but he offered no greeting. A woman joined him, and the two, quite passive, waited to discover my intentions.

Eat I must, so I stepped forward and asked if I could have a meal. Without stirring, the man gave a sullen assent. Could I have food at once? Yes, in a few minutes. Would they show me—the dining-room? Man and woman turned upon their heels, and I followed. The entrance led into a filthy kitchen; out of this I turned to the right, went along a passage upon which opened certain chamber doors, and was conducted into a room at the end—for the nonce, a dining-room, but at ordinary times a bedroom. Evidently the kitchen served for native guests; as a foreigner I was treated with more ceremony. Left alone till my meal should be ready, I examined the surroundings. The floor was of worn stone, which looked to me like the natural foundation of the house; the walls were rudely plastered, cracked, grimed, and with many a deep chink; as for the window, it admitted light, but, owing to the aged dirt which had gathered upon it, refused any view of things without save in two or three places where the glass was broken; by these apertures, and at every point of the framework, entered a sharp wind. In one corner stood an iron bedstead, with mattress and bedding in a great roll upon it; a shaky deal table and primitive chair completed the furniture. Ornament did not wholly lack; round the walls hung a number of those coloured political caricatures (several indecent) which are published by some Italian newspapers, and a large advertisement of a line of emigrant ships between Naples and New York. Moreover, there was suspended in a corner a large wooden crucifix, very quaint, very hideous, and black with grime.

Spite of all this, I still debated with myself whether to engage the room for the night. I should have liked to stay; the thought of a sunny morning here on the height strongly allured me, and it seemed a shame to confess myself beaten by an Italian inn. On the other hand, the look of the people did not please me; they had surly, forbidding faces. I glanced at the door—no lock. Fears, no doubt, were ridiculous; yet I felt ill at ease. I would decide after seeing the sort of fare that was set before me.

The meal came with no delay. First, a dish of great *peperoni* cut up in oil. This gorgeous fruit is never much to my taste, but I had as yet eaten no such *peperoni* as those of Squillace; an hour or two afterwards my mouth was still burning from the heat of a few morsels to which I was constrained by hunger. Next appeared a dish for which I had covenanted—the only food, indeed, which the people had been able to offer at short notice—a stew of pork and potatoes. Pork (*majale*) is the staple meat of all this region; viewing it as Homeric diet, I had often battened upon such flesh with moderate satisfaction. But the pork of Squillace defeated me; it smelt abominably, and it was tough as leather. No eggs were to be had, no macaroni; cheese, yes—the familiar *cacio cavallo*. Bread appeared in the form of a flat circular cake, a foot in diameter, with a hole through the middle; its consistency resembled that of cold pancake. And the drink! At least I might hope to solace myself with an honest draught of red wine. I poured from the thick decanter (dirtier vessel was never seen on table) and tasted. The stuff was poison. Assuredly I am far from fastidious; this, I believe, was the only occasion when wine has been offered me in Italy which I could not drink. After desperately trying to persuade myself that the liquor was merely "rough", that its nauseating flavour meant only a certain coarse quality of the local grape, I began to suspect that it was largely mixed with water—the water of Squillace! Notwithstanding a severe thirst, I could not and durst not drink.

Very soon I made my way to the kitchen, where my driver, who had stabled his horses, sat feeding heartily; he looked up with his merry smile, surprised at the rapidity with which I had finished. How I envied his sturdy stomach! With the remark that I was going to have a stroll round the town and should be back to settle things in half an hour, I hastened into the open.

15
Miseria

"WHAT do people do here?" I once asked at a little town between Rome and Naples; and the man with whom I talked, shrugging his shoulders, answered curtly, "*C'è miseria*"—there's nothing but poverty.[1] The same reply would be given in towns and villages without number throughout the length of Italy. I had seen poverty enough, and squalid conditions of life, but the most ugly and repulsive collection of houses I ever came upon was the town of Squillace. I admit the depressing effect of rain and cloud, and of hunger worse than unsatisfied; these things count emphatically in my case; but under no conditions could inhabited Squillace be other than an offence to eye and nostril. The houses are, with one or two exceptions, ground-floor hovels; scarce a weather-tight dwelling is discoverable; the general impression is that of dilapidated squalor. Streets, in the ordinary sense of the word, do not exist; irregular alleys climb about the rugged heights, often so steep as to be difficult of ascent; here and there a few boulders have been thrown together to afford a footing, and in some places the native rock lies bare; but for the most part one walks on the accumulated filth of ages. At the moment of my visit there was in progress the only kind of cleaning which Squillace knows; down every trodden way and every intermural gully poured a flush of rain-water, with occasionally a leaping torrent or small cascade, which all but barred progress. Open doors everywhere allowed me a glimpse of the domestic arrangements, and I saw that my albergo had some reason to pride itself on superiority; life in a country called civilized cannot easily be more primitive than under these crazy roofs. As for the people, they had a dull, heavy aspect; rare as must be the apparition of a foreigner among them, no one showed the slightest curiosity as I passed, and (an honourable feature of the district) no one begged. Women went about in the rain protected by a shawl-like garment of very picturesque colouring; it had broad yellow stripes on a red ground, the tones subdued to a warm richness.

Ruins of the Convent and Church of Santa Chiara

The animal population was not without its importance. Turn where I would I encountered lean, black pigs, snouting, frisking, scampering, and squealing as if the bad weather were a delight to them. Gaunt, low-spirited dogs prowled about in search of food, and always ran away at my approach. In one precipitous byway, where the air was insupportably foul, I came upon an odd little scene: a pig and a cat, quite alone, were playing together, and enjoying themselves with remarkable spirit. The pig lay down in the running mud, and pussy, having leapt on to him, began to scratch his back, bite his ears, stroke his sides. Suddenly, porker was uppermost and the cat, pretending to struggle for life, under his forefeet. It was the only amusing incident I met with at Squillace, and the sole instance of anything like cheerful vitality.

Above the habitations stand those prominent ruins which had held my eye during our long ascent. These are the rugged walls and windows of a monastery[2], not old enough to possess much interest, and, on the crowning height, the heavy remnants of a Norman castle, with one fine doorway still intact.[3] Bitterly I deplored the gloomy sky which spoiled what would else have been a magnificent view from this point of vantage—a view wide-spreading in all directions, with Sila northwards, Aspromonte to the south, and between them a long horizon of the sea. Looking down upon Squillace, one sees its houses niched among huge masses of granite, which protrude from the scanty soil, or clinging to the rocky surface like limpet shells. Was this the site of Scylaceum, or is it, as some hold, merely a mediæval refuge which took the name of the old city nearer to the coast?[4] The Scylaceum of the sixth century is described by Cassiodorus—a

Entrance to the Norman castle

picture glowing with admiration and tenderness. It lay, he says, upon the side of a hill; nay, it hung there "like a cluster of grapes", in such glorious light and warmth that, to his mind, it deserved to be called the native region of the sun. The fertility of the country around was unexampled; nowhere did earth yield to mortals a more luxurious life. Quoting this description, Lenormant holds that, with due regard to time's changes, it exactly fits the site of Squillace.[5] Yet Cassiodorus says that the hill by which you approached the town was not high enough to weary a traveller, a consideration making for the later view that Scylaceum stood very near to the Marina of Catanzaro, at a spot called Roccella, where not only is the nature of the ground suitable, but there exist considerable traces of ancient building, such as are not discoverable here on the mountain top. Lenormant thought that Roccella was merely the sea-port of the inland town. I wish he were right. No archæologist, whose work I have studied, affects me with such a personal charm, with such a sense of intellectual sympathy, as François Lenormant—dead, alas, before he could complete his delightful book.[6] But one fears that, in this instance, he judged too hastily.

There is no doubt, fortunately, as to the position of the religious house founded by Cassiodorus; it was in the shadow of Mons Moscius, and quite near to the sea. I had marked the spot during my drive up the valley, and now saw it again from this far height, but I could not be satisfied with distant views. Weather and evil quarters making it impossible to remain at Squillace, I decided to drive forthwith to the railway station, see how much time remained to me before the arrival of the train for Reggio, and, if it could be managed, visit in that interval the place that attracted me.

It is my desire to be at peace with all men, and in Italy I have rarely failed to part with casual acquaintances—even innkeepers and cocchieri—on friendly terms; but my host of the *Albergo Nazionale* made it difficult to preserve good humour. Not only did he charge thrice the reasonable sum for the meal I could not eat, but his bill for my driver's *colazione* contained such astonishing items that I had to question the lad as to what he had really consumed. It proved to be a very ugly case of extortion, and the tone of sullen menace with which my arguments were met did not help to smooth things. Presently the man hit upon a pleasant sort of compromise. Why, he asked, did I not pay the bill as it stood, and then, on dismissing my carriage—he had learnt that I was not returning to Catanzaro—deduct as much as I chose from the payment of the driver? A pretty piece of rascality, this, which he would certainly not have suggested but that the driver was a mere boy, helpless himself and bound to render an account to his master. I had to be content with resolutely striking off half the sum charged for the lad's wine (he was supposed to have drunk about four litres), and sending the receipted bill to Don Pasquale at Catanzaro, that he might be ready with information if any future traveller consulted him about the accommodation to be had at Squillace.[7] No one is likely to do so for a long time to come, but I have no doubt Don Pasquale had a chuckle of amused indignation over the interesting and very dirty bit of paper. We drove quickly down the winding road, and from below I again admired the picturesqueness of Squillace. Both my guide-books, by the way, the orthodox English and German authorities, assert that from the railway station by the seashore Squillace is invisible.[8] Which of the two borrowed this information from the other? As a matter of fact, the view of mountain and town from the station platform is admirable, though, of course, at so great a distance, only a whitish patch represents the hovels and ruins upon their royal height.

I found that I had a good couple of hours at my disposal, and that to the foot of Mons Moscius (now called Coscia di Stalletti) was only a short walk. It rained drearily, but by this time I had ceased to think of the weather. After watching the carriage for a moment, as it rolled away on the long road back to Catanzaro (sorry not to be going with it), I followed the advice of the stationmaster, and set out to walk along the line of rails towards the black, furrowed mountain side.

16
Cassiodorus

THE iron way crosses the mouth of the valley river. As I had already noticed, it was a turbid torrent, of dull yellow; where it poured into the sea, it made a vast, clean-edged patch of its own hue upon the darker surface of the waves. This peculiarity resulted, no doubt, from much rain upon the hills; it may be that in calmer seasons the Fiume di Squillace bears more resemblance to the Pellena as one pictures it, a delightful stream flowing through the gardens of the old monastery. Cassiodorus tells us that it abounded in fish. One of his happy labours was to make fish-ponds, filled and peopled from the river itself. In the cliffside where Mons Moscius breaks above the shore are certain rocky caves, and by some it is thought that, in speaking of his fish-preserves, Cassiodorus refers to these. Whatever the local details, it was from this feature that the house took its name, Monasterium Vivariense.[1]

Here, then, I stood in full view of the spot which I had so often visioned in my mind's eye. Much of the land hereabout—probably an immense tract of hill and valley—was the old monk's patrimonial estate. We can trace his family back through three generations, to a Cassiodorus[2], an Illustris of the falling Western Empire, who about the middle of the fifth century defended his native Bruttii against an invasion of the Vandals. The grandson of this noble was a distinguished man all through the troubled time which saw Italy pass under the dominion of Odovacar, and under the conquest of Theodoric; the Gothic king raised him to the supreme office of Prætorian Prefect. We learn that he had great herds of horses, bred in the Bruttian forests, and that Theodoric was indebted to him for the mounting of troops of cavalry. He and his ancestry would signify little now-a-days but for the life-work of his greater son—Magnus Aurelius Cassiodorus Senator, statesman, historian, monk. *Senator* was not a title, but a personal name; the name our Cassiodorus always used when speaking of himself. But history calls him otherwise, and for us he must be Cassiodorus still.[3]

The year of his birth was 480. In the same year were born two other men, glories of their age, whose fame is more generally remembered: Boethius the poet and philosopher, and Benedict called Saint.[4]

From Quæstorship (old name with no longer the old significance) to Prætorian Prefecture, Cassiodorus held all offices of state, and seems under every proof to have shown the nobler qualities of statesmanship. During his ripe years he stood by the side of Theodoric[5], minister in prime trust, doubtless helping to shape that wise and benevolent policy which made the reign of the Ostrogoth a time of rest and hope for the Italian people—Roman no longer; the word had lost its meaning, though not its magic. The Empire of the West had perished; Theodoric and his minister, clearly understanding this, and resolute against the Byzantine claim which was but in half abeyance, aimed at the creation of an independent Italy, where Goth and Latin should blend into a new race. The hope proved vain. Theodoric's successors, no longer kings, but mere Gothic chieftains, strove obscurely against inevitable doom, until the generals of Justinian trod Italy into barren servitude. Only when the purpose of his life was shattered, when—Theodoric long dead—his still faithful service to the Gothic rule became an idle form, when Belisarius was compassing the royal city of Ravenna, and voice of council could no longer make itself heard amid tumult and ruin, did Cassiodorus retire from useless office, and turn his back upon the world.

He was aged about sixty. Long before, he had written a history of the Goths[6] (known to us only in a compendium by another hand), of which the purpose seems to have been to reconcile the Romans to the Gothic monarchy; it began by endeavouring to prove that Goths had fought against the Greeks at Troy. Now that his public life was over, he published a collection of the state papers composed by him under the Gothic rulers from Theodoric to Vitigis[7]: for the most part royal rescripts addressed to foreign powers and to officials of the kingdom. Invaluable for their light upon men and things fourteen hundred years ago, these *Variæ* of Cassiodorus; and for their own sake, as literary productions, most characteristic, most entertaining. Not quite easy to read, for the Latin is by no means Augustan, but, after labour well spent, a delightful revelation of the man and the age. Great is the variety of subjects dealt with or touched upon; from the diplomatic relations between Ravenna and Constantinople[8], or the alliances of the Amal line with barbaric royalties in Gaul and Africa, to the pensioning of an aged charioteer and the domestic troubles of a small landowner. We form a good general idea of the condition of Italy at that time, and, on many points political and social, gather a fund of most curious detail. The world shown to us is in some respects highly civilized, its civilization still that of Rome, whose laws, whose manners, have in great part survived the Teutonic conquest; from another point of view it is a mere world of ruin, possessed by triumphant barbarism, and sinking to intellectual darkness. We note the decay of central power, and the growth of political anarchy; we observe the process by which Roman nobles, the Senatorial Order when a Senate lingers only in name, are becoming the turbulent lords of the Middle Ages, each a power in his own territory, levying private war, scornful of public interests. The city of Rome has little part in this turbid history, yet her name is never mentioned without reverence, and in theory she is still the centre of the world. Glimpses are granted us of her fallen majesty; we learn that Theodoric exerted himself to preserve her noble buildings, to restore her monuments; at the same time we hear of marble stolen from palaces in decay, and of temples which, as private property, are converted to ignoble use. Moreover, at Rome sits an ecclesiastical dignitary, known as *Papa*, to whose doings already attaches considerable importance. One of the last acts of the Senate which had any real meaning was to make a decree with regard to the election of this Bishop, forbidding his advance by the way of simony. Theodoric, an Arian, interferes only with the Church of Rome in so far as public peace demands it. In one of his letters occurs a most remarkable dictum on the subject of toleration. "*Religionem imperare non possumus, quia nemo cogitur ut credat invitus*— we cannot impose a religious faith, for no one can be compelled to believe against his conscience."[9] This must, of course, have been the king's own sentiment, but Cassiodorus worded it, and doubtless with approval.

Indeed, we are at no loss to discern the mind of the secretary in these official papers.[10] Cassiodorus speaks as often for himself as for the king; he delights to expatiate, from an obviously personal point of view, on any subject that interests him. One of these is natural history; give him but the occasion, and he gossips of beasts, birds, and fishes, in a flow of the most genial impertinence. Certain bronze elephants on the Via Sacra are falling to pieces and must be repaired: in giving the order, Theodoric's minister pens a little treatise on the habits and characteristics of the elephant. His erudition is often displayed: having to convey some direction about the Circus at Rome, he begins with a pleasant sketch of the history of chariot racing. One marvels at the man who, in such a period, preserved this mood of liberal leisure. His style is perfectly suited to the matter; diffuse, ornate, amusingly affected; altogether a *precious* mode of writing, characteristic of literary decadence. When the moment demands it, he is pompously grandiloquent; in dealing with a delicate situation, he becomes involved and obscure. We perceive in him a born courtier, a proud noble, a statesman of high purpose and no little sagacity; therewith, many gracious and attractive qualities, coloured by weaknesses, such as agreeable pedantry and amiable self-esteem, which are in part personal, partly the note of his time.

One's picture of the man is, of course, completed from a knowledge of the latter years of his life, of the works produced during his monastic retirement. Christianity rarely finds expression in the *Variæ*, a point sufficiently explained by the Gothic heresy, which imposed discretion in public utterances; on the other hand, pagan mythology abounds; we observe the hold it still had upon educated minds—education, indeed, meaning much the same thing in the sixth century after Christ as in the early times of the Empire. Cassiodorus can never have been a fanatical devotee of any creed. Of his sincere piety there is no doubt; it appears in a vast commentary on the Psalms, and more clearly in the book he wrote for the guidance and edification of his brother monks—brothers (*carissimi fratres*), for in his humility he declined to become the Abbot of Vivariense; enough that his worldly dignity, his spiritual and mental graces, assured to him the influence he desired. The notable characteristic of his rule was a sanctifying of intellectual labour. In abandoning the world, he by no means renounced his interest in its civilization. Statesmanship having failed to stem the tide of Oriental tyranny and northern barbarism, he set himself to save as much as possible of the nobler part, to secure for happier ages the record of human attainment. Great was the importance he attached to the work of his Antiquarii—copyists who laboured to preserve the manuscript literature which was in danger of utterly perishing. With special reference to their work upon the Scriptures, he tells them that they "fight against the wiles of Satan with pen and ink." And again: "Writing with three fingers, they thus symbolize the virtues of the Holy Trinity; using a reed, they thus attack the craft of the Devil with that very instrument which smote the Lord's head in his Passion."[11] But all literature was his care. That the copyist might write correctly, he digested the works of half a dozen grammarians into a treatise on orthography. Further, that the books of the monastery might wear "a wedding garment" (his own phrase), he designed a great variety of bindings, which were kept as patterns.

There, at the foot of Moscius, did these brethren and their founder live and work. But on the top of the mountain was another retreat, known as Castellense, for those monks who—*divina gratia suffragante*—desired a severer discipline, and left the cœnobitic house to become anchorites. Did these virtuous brothers continue their literary labours? One hopes so, and one is glad that Cassiodorus himself seems to have ended his life down in the valley by the Pellena.

A third class of monks finds mention, those in whom "*Frigidus obstiterit circum præcordia sanguis,*" quotes the founder. In other words, the hopelessly stupid. For these there was labour in the garden, and to console them Cassiodorus recites from a Psalm: "Thou shalt eat the labour of thy hands; happy shalt thou be, and it shall be well with thee."[12] A smile is on the countenance of the humane brother. He did his utmost indeed, for the comfort, as well as the spiritual welfare, of his community. Baths were built "for the sick" (heathendom had been cleaner, but we must not repine); for the suffering, too, and for pilgrims, exceptional food was provided—young pigeons, delicate fish, fruit, honey; a new kind of lamp was invented, to burn for long hours without attention; dials and clepsydras marked the progress of day and night.

Among the monastic duties is that of giving instruction to the peasantry round about. They are not to be oppressed, these humble tillers of the soil, for is it not written that "My yoke is easy, and my burden is light"?[13] But one must insist that they come frequently to religious service, and that they do not *lucos colere*—worship in groves—which shows that a heathen mind still lingered among the people, and that they reverenced the old deities. Benedict, the contemporary of Cassiodorus (we have no authority for supposing that they knew each other), when he first ascended the mount above Casinum, found a temple of Apollo, with the statue of the god receiving daily homage. Archæologists have tried to determine at what date the old religion became extinct in Italy. Their search leads them well into the Middle Ages, but, undoubtedly, even then they pause too soon.

Legend says that Cassiodorus attained the age of nearly a hundred years. We may be sure that to the end he lived busily, for of idleness he speaks with abhorrence as the root of evil. Doubtless he was always a copious talker, and to many a pilgrim he must have gossiped delightfully, alternating mundane memories with counsel good for the soul. Only one of his monastic brethren is known to us as a man of any distinction: this was Dionysius Exiguus, or the Little, by birth a Scythian, a man of much learning.[14] He compiled the first history of the

Councils, and, a matter more important, originated the computation of the Christian Era; for up to this time men had dated in the old way, by shadowy consulships and confusing Indictions. There is happy probability that Cassiodorus lived out his life in peace; but the monastery did not long exist; like that of Benedict on Monte Cassino, it seems to have been destroyed by the Lombards, savages and Arians.[15] No trace of it remains. But high up on the mountain is a church known as S. Maria de Vetere, a name indicating an ancient foundation, which perhaps was no other than the anchorite house of Castellense.

17
The Grotta

ABOUT a mile beyond Squillace the line passes by a tunnel through the promontory of Mons Moscius. At this point on the face of the seacliff I was told that I should discover a *grotta,* one of the caverns which some think are indicated by Cassiodorus when he speaks of his fish-preserves. Arrived near the mouth of the tunnel I found a signal-box, where several railway men were grouped in talk; to them I addressed myself, and all immediately turned to offer me guidance. We had to clamber down a rocky descent, and skirt the waves for a few yards; when my cluster of companions had sufficiently shown their goodwill, all turned back but one, who made a point of giving me safe conduct into the cave itself. He was a bronzed, bright-eyed, happy-looking fellow of middle age, his humorous intelligence appearing in a flow of gossip about things local. We entered a narrow opening, some twelve feet high, which ran perhaps twenty yards into the cliff. Lenormant supposes that this was a quarry made by the original Greek colonists.[1] If Cassiodorus used it for the purpose mentioned, the cave must have been in direct communication either with the sea or the river; at present, many yards of sloping shingle divide it from the line of surf, and the river flows far away. Movement of the shore there has of course been, and the Pellena may have considerably changed the direction of its outflow; our author's description being but vague, one can only muse on probabilities and likelihoods.

Whilst we talked, the entrance to the cave was shadowed, and there entered one of the men who had turned back at half-way; his face betrayed the curiosity which had after all prevailed to bring him hither. Shouting merrily, my companion hailed him as "Brigadiere". The two friends contrasted very amusingly; for the brigadiere was a mild, timid, simple creature, who spoke with diffidence; he kept his foolishly good-natured eyes fixed upon me, a gaze of wonder. After listening to all that my guide had to say—it was nothing to the point, dealing chiefly with questions of railway engineering—I had just begun to explain my interest in the locality, and I mentioned the name of Cassiodorus. As it passed my lips the jovial fellow burst into a roar of laughter. "Cassiodorio![2] Ha, ha! Cassiodorio! Ha, ha, ha!" I asked him what he meant, and found that he was merely delighted to hear a stranger unexpectedly utter a name in familiar local use. He ran out from the cave, and pointed up the valley; yonder was a fountain which bore the name "Fontana di Cassiodorio".[3] (From my authors I knew of this; it may or may not have genuine historic interest.) Thereupon, I tried to discover whether any traditions hung to the name, but these informants had only a vague idea that Cassiodorus was a man of times long gone by. How, they questioned in turn, did I know anything about him? Why, from books, I replied; among them books which the ancient himself had written more than a thousand years ago. This was too much for the brigadiere; it moved him to stammered astonishment. Did I mean to say that books written more than a thousand years ago still existed? The jovial friend, good-naturedly scornful, cried out that of course they did, and added with triumphant air that they were not in the language of to-day, but in *latino, latino!* All this came as a revelation to the other, who

stared and marvelled, never taking his eyes from my face. At length he
burst out with an emphatic question; these same books, were they large?
Why yes, I answered, some of them. Were they—were they *as large as a
missal?* A shout of jolly laughter interrupted us. It seemed to me that my
erudite companion was in the habit of getting fun out of his friend the
brigadiere, but so kindly did he look and speak, that it must have been
difficult for the simpleton ever to take offence.

Meanwhile the sullen sky had grown blacker, and rain was
descending heavily. In any case, I should barely have had time to go
further, and had to be content with a description from my companions
of a larger cave some distance beyond this, which is known as the Grotta
of San Gregorio—with reference, no doubt, to S. Gregory the
Thaumaturgist[4]; to him was dedicated a Greek monastery, built on the
ruined site of Vivariense. After the Byzantine conquest of the sixth
century, Magna Græcia once more justified its ancient name; the
civilization of this region became purely Greek; but for the Lombards
and ecclesiastical Rome, perhaps no Latin Italy would have survived.
Greek monks, who through the darkest age were skilful copyists,
continued in Calabria the memorable work of Cassiodorus. The ninth
century saw Saracen invasion, and then it was, no doubt, that the second
religious house under Mons Moscius perished from its place.

Thinking over this, I walked away from the cave and climbed again
to the railway; my friends also were silent and ruminative. Not
unnaturally, I suspected that a desire for substantial thanks had some
part in their silence, and at a convenient spot I made suitable offering.
It was done, I trust, with all decency, for I knew that I had the better
kind of Calabrian to deal with; but neither the jovially intelligent man
nor the pleasant simpleton would for a moment entertain this
suggestion. They refused with entire dignity—grave, courteous, firm—
and as soon as I had apologized, which I did not without emphasis, we
were on the same terms as before; with handshaking, we took kindly
leave of each other. Such self-respect is the rarest thing in Italy south of
Rome, but in Calabria I found it more than once.

By when I had walked back to the station, hunger exhausted me.
There was no buffet, and seemingly no place in the neighbourhood
where food could be purchased, but on my appealing to the porter I

learnt that he was accustomed to entertain stray travellers in his house hard-by, whither he at once led me. To describe the room where my meal was provided would be sheer ingratitude: in my recollection it compares favourably with the *Albergo Nazionale* of Squillace. I had bread, salame, cheese, and, heaven be thanked, wine that I could swallow—nay, for here sounds the note of thanklessness, it was honest wine, of which I drank freely. Honest, too, the charge that was made; I should have felt cheap at ten times the price that sudden accession of bodily and mental vigour. Luck be with him, serviceable *facchino* of Squillace![5] I remember his human face, and his smile of pleasure when I declared all he modestly set before me good and good again. His hospitality sent me on my way rejoicing—glad that I had seen the unspeakable little mountain town, thrice glad that I had looked upon Mons Moscius and trodden by the river Pellena. Rain fell in torrents, but I no longer cared. When presently the train arrived, I found a comfortable corner, and looked forward with a restful sigh to the seven hours' travel which would bring me into view of Sicily.

In the carriage sat a school-boy, a book open upon his knee. When our eyes had met twice or thrice, and an ingenuous smile rose to his handsome face, I opened conversation, and he told me that he came every day to school from a little place called San Sostene to Catanzaro, there being no nearer instruction above the elementary; a journey of some sixteen miles each way, and not to be reckoned by English standards, for it meant changing at the Marina for the valley train, and finally going up the mountain side by *diligenza*. The lad flushed with delight in his adventure—a real adventure for him to meet with some one from far-off England. Just before we stopped at San Sostene, he presented me with his card—why had he a card?—which bore the name, De Luca Fedele.[6] A bright and spirited lad, who seemed to have the best qualities of his nation; I wish I might live to hear him spoken of as a man doing honour to Italy.

At this station another travelling companion took the school-boy's place; a priest, who soon addressed me in courteous talk.[7] He journeyed only for a short way, and, when alighting, pointed skyward through the dark (night had fallen) to indicate his mountain parish miles inland. He, too, offered me his card, adding a genial invitation; I found he was

Parroco (parish priest) of San Nicolà at Badolato. I would ask nothing better than to visit him, some autumn-tide, when grapes are ripening above the Ionian Sea.

It was a wild night. When the rain at length ceased, lightning flashed ceaselessly about the dark heights of Aspromonte; later, the moon rose, and, sailing amid grandly illumined clouds, showed white waves rolling in upon the beach. Wherever the train stopped, that sea-music was in my ears—now seeming to echo a verse of Homer, now the softer rhythm of Theocritus. Think of what one may in day-time on this far southern shore, its nights are sacred to the poets of Hellas. In rounding Cape Spartivento, I strained my eyes through the moonlight—unhappily a waning moon, which had shone with full orb the evening I ascended to Catanzaro—to see the Sicilian mountains; at length they stood up darkly against the paler night. There came back to my memory a voyage at glorious sunrise, years ago, when I passed through the Straits of Messina, and all day long gazed at Etna, until its cone, solitary upon the horizon, shone faint and far in the glow of evening—the morrow to bring me a first sight of Greece.

Reggio Calabria
rso G. Garibaldi e Palazzo Munici

18
Reggio

BY its natural situation Reggio is marked for an unquiet history. It was a gateway of Magna Græcia; it lay straight in the track of conquering Rome when she moved towards Sicily; it offered points of strategic importance to every invader or defender of the peninsula throughout the mediæval wars. Goth and Saracen, Norman, Teuton and Turk, seized, pillaged, and abandoned, each in turn, this stronghold overlooking the narrow sea.[1] Then the earthquakes, ever menacing between Vesuvius and Etna; that of 1783, which wrought destruction throughout Calabria, laid Reggio in ruins, so that to-day it has the aspect of a newly-built city[2], curving its regular streets, amphitheatre-wise, upon the slope that rises between shore and mountain. Of Rhegium little is discernible above ground; of the ages that followed scarce anything remains but the Norman fortress, so shaken by that century-old disaster³ that huge gaps show where its rent wall sank to a lower level upon the hillside.

At first, one has eyes and thoughts for nothing but the landscape. From the terrace road along the shore, Via Plutino, beauties and glories indescribable lie before one at every turn of the head. Aspromonte, with its forests and crags; the shining straits, sail-dotted, opening to a sea-horizon north and south; and, on the other side, the mountain-island, crowned with snow. Hours long I stood and walked here, marvelling delightedly at all I saw, but in the end ever fixing my gaze on Sicily. Clouds passed across the blue sky, and their shadows upon the Sicilian panorama made ceaseless change of hue and outline. At early morning I saw the crest of Etna glistening as the first sun-ray smote upon its white ridges; at fall of day, the summit hidden by heavy clouds, and western beams darting from behind the mountain, those far, cold heights glimmered with a hue of palest emerald, seeming but a vision of the sunset heaven, translucent, ever about to vanish. Night transformed but did not all conceal. Yonder, a few miles away, shone the harbour and the streets of Messina, and many a gleaming point along the island coast, strand-touching or high above, signalled the homes of men. Calm, warm, and clear, this first night at Reggio; I could not turn away from the siren-voice of the waves; hearing scarce a footstep but my own, I paced hither and thither by the sea-wall, alone with memories.

The rebuilding of Reggio has made it clean and sweet; its air is blended from that of mountain and sea, ever renewed, delicate and inspiriting. But, apart from the harbour, one notes few signs of activity; the one long street, Corso Garibaldi, has little traffic; most of the shops close shortly after nightfall, and then there is no sound of wheels; all would be perfectly still but for the occasional cry of lads who sell newspapers. Indeed, the town is strangely quiet, considering its size and aspect of importance; one has to search for a restaurant, and I doubt if more than one café exists. At my hotel⁴ the dining-room was a public *trattoria*, opening upon the street, but only two or three military men— the eternal officers—made use of it, and I felt a less cheery social atmosphere than at Taranto or at Catanzaro. One recurring incident did not tend to exhilarate. Sitting in view of a closed door, I saw children's faces pressed against the glass, peering little faces, which sought a

The Corso Garibaldi, c. 1900

favourable moment; suddenly the door would open, and there sounded a thin voice, begging for *un pezzo di pane*—a bit of bread. Whenever the waiter caught sight of these little mendicants, he rushed out with simulated fury, and pursued them along the pavement. I have no happy recollection of my Reggian meals.

An interesting feature of the streets is the frequency of carved inscriptions, commemorating citizens who died in their struggle for liberty. Amid quiet byways, for instance, I discovered a tablet with the name of a young soldier who fell at that spot, fighting against the Bourbon, in 1860: "*offerse per l'unità della patria sua vita quadrilustre.*"[5] The very insignificance of this young life makes the fact more touching; one thinks of the unnumbered lives sacrificed upon this soil, age after age, to the wild-beast instinct of mankind, and how pathetic the attempt to preserve the memory of one boy, so soon to become a meaningless name! His own voice seems to plead with us for a regretful thought, to speak from the stone in sad arraignment of tyranny and bloodshed. A voice which has no accent of hope. In the days to come, as through all time that is past, man will lord it over his fellow, and earth will be stained red from veins of young and old. That sweet and sounding name of *patria* becomes an illusion and a curse; linked with the pretentious modernism, *civilization,* it serves as plea to the latter-day barbarian, ravening and reckless under his civil garb. How can one greatly wish for the consolidation and prosperity of Italy, knowing that national vigour tends more and more to international fear and hatred? They who perished that Italy might be born again, dreamt of other things than old savagery clanging in new weapons. In our day there is but one Italian patriot; he who tills the soil, and sows, and reaps, ignorant or careless of all beyond his furrowed field.[6]

Whilst I was still thinking of that memorial tablet, I found myself in front of the Cathedral. As a structure it makes small appeal, dating only from the seventeenth century, and heavily restored in times more recent; but the first sight of the façade is strangely stirring. For across the whole front, in great letters which one who runs may read, is carved a line from the Acts of the Apostles:—

"Circumlegentes devenimus Rhegium." [7]

Save only those sonorous words which circle the dome of S. Peter's, I have seen no inscription on Christian temple which seemed to me so impressive. "We fetched a compass, and came to Rhegium." Paul was on his voyage from Cæsarea to Rome, and here his ship touched, here at the haven beneath Aspromonte. The fact is familiar enough, but, occupied as I was with other thoughts, it had not yet occurred to me; the most pious pilgrim of an earlier day could not have felt himself more strongly arrested than I when I caught sight of these words. Were I to inhabit Reggio, I

The Cathedral as it was before the earthquake of 1908

should never pass the Cathedral without stopping to read and think; the carving would never lose its power over my imagination. It unites for me two elements of moving interest: a vivid fact from the ancient world, recorded in the music of the ancient tongue. All day the words rang in my head, even as at Rome I have gone about murmuring to myself: "*Aedificabo ecclesiam meam.*"[8] What a noble solemnity in this Latin speech! And how vast the historic significance of such monumental words! Moralize who will; enough for me to hear with delight that deep-toned harmony, and to thrill with the strangeness of old things made new.

It was Sunday, which at Reggio is a day of market. Crowds of country-folk had come into the town with the produce of field and garden; all the open spaces were occupied with temporary stalls; at hand stood innumerable donkeys, tethered till business should be over. The produce exhibited was of very fine quality, especially the vegetables; I noticed cauliflowers measuring more than a foot across the white. Of costume there was little to be observed—though the long soft cap worn by most of the men, hanging bag-like over one ear almost to the shoulder, is picturesque. The female water-carriers, a long slim cask resting lengthwise upon their padded heads, hold attention as they go to and from the fountains. Good-looking people, grave of manner, and doing their business without noise. It was my last sight of the Calabrian hillsmen; to the end they held my interest and my respect. When towns have sucked dry their population of strength and virtue, it is such as these, hardy from the free breath of heaven and the scent of earth, who will renew a flaccid race.

Walking beyond the town in the southern direction, where the shape of Etna shows more clearly amid the lower mountains, I found myself approaching what looked like a handsome public edifice, a museum or gallery of art. It was a long building, graced with a portico, and coloured effectively in dull red; all about it stood lemon trees, and behind, overtopping the roof, several fine palms. Moved by curiosity I quickened my steps, and as I drew nearer I felt sure that this must be some interesting institution of which I had not heard. Presently I observed along the façade a row of heads of oxen carved in stone—an ornament decidedly puzzling. Last of all my eyes perceived, over the stately

entrance, the word "Macello", and with astonishment I became aware that this fine structure, so agreeably situated, was nothing else than the town slaughterhouse. Does the like exist elsewhere? It was a singular bit of advanced civilization, curiously out of keeping with the thoughts which had occupied me on my walk. Why, I wonder, has Reggio paid such exceptional attention to this department of its daily life? One did not quite know whether to approve this frank exhibition of carnivorous zeal; obviously something can be said in its favour, yet, on the other hand, a man who troubles himself with finer scruples would perhaps choose not to be reminded of pole-axe and butcher's knife, preferring that such things should shun the light of day. It gave me, for the moment, an odd sense of having strayed into the world of those romancers who forecast the future; a slaughterhouse of tasteful architecture, set in a grove of lemon trees and date palms, suggested the dreamy ideal of some reformer whose palate shrinks from vegetarianism. To my mind this had no place amid the landscape which spread about me. It checked my progress; I turned abruptly, to lose the impression as soon as possible.

No such trouble has been taken to provide comely housing for the collection of antiquities which the town possesses.[9] The curator who led me through the museum (of course I was the sole visitor[10]) lamented that it was only communal, the Italian Government not having yet cared to take it under control; he was an enthusiast, and spoke with feeling of the time and care he had spent upon these precious relics—*sedici anni di vita*—sixteen years of life, and, after all, who cared for them? There was a little library of archæological works, which contained two volumes only of the *Corpus Inscriptionum Latinarum*[11]; who, asked the curator sadly, would supply money to purchase the rest? Place had been found on the walls for certain modern pictures of local interest. One represented a pasture on the heights of Aspromonte, shepherds and their cattle amid rich herbage, under a summer sky, with purple summits enclosing them on every side; the other, also a Calabrian mountain scene, but sternly grand in the light of storm; a dark tarn, a rushing torrent, the lonely wilderness. Naming the painter, my despondent companion shook his head, and sighed "*Morto! Morto!*"[12]

Ere I left, the visitors' book was opened for my signature. Some twenty pages only had been covered since the founding of the museum, and most of the names were German. Fortunately, I glanced at the beginning, and there, on the first page, was written: "François Lenormant, Membre de l'Institut de France"—the date, 1882. The small, delicate character was very suggestive of the man as I conceived him; to come upon his name thus unexpectedly gave me a thrill of pleasure; it was like being brought of a sudden into the very presence of

Reggio Museum: Gissing's signature
in the visitors' book

him whose spirit had guided, instructed, borne me delightful company throughout my wanderings. When I turned to the curator, and spoke of this discovery, sympathy at once lighted up his face. Yes, yes! He remembered the visit; he had the clearest recollection of Lenormant— "*un bravo giovane!*"[13] Thereupon, he directed my attention to a little slip of paper pasted into the inner cover of the book, on which were written in pencil a few Greek letters; they were from the hand of Lenormant himself, who had taken out his pencil to illustrate something he was saying about a Greek inscription in the museum. Carefully had this scrap been preserved by the good curator; his piety touched and delighted me.

I could have desired no happier incident for the close of my journey; by lucky chance this visit to the museum had been postponed till the last morning, and, as I idled through the afternoon about the Via Plutino[14], my farewell mood was in full harmony with that in which I had landed from Naples upon the Calabrian shore. So hard a thing to catch and to retain, the mood corresponding perfectly to an intellectual bias—hard, at all events, for him who cannot shape his life as he will, and whom circumstance ever menaces with dreary harassment. Alone and quiet, I heard the washing of the waves; I saw the evening fall on cloud-wreathed Etna, the twinkling lights come forth upon Scylla and Charybdis; and, as I looked my last towards the Ionian Sea, I wished it were mine to wander endlessly amid the silence of the ancient world, to-day and all its sounds forgotten.

THE END

NOTES

CHAPTER 1: FROM NAPLES

1   On 11 November 1897 Gissing obtained from the booksellers Detken
     & Co. the address of an Italian family who let rooms. He stayed for a few
     days with Signor and Signora Labriola, Chiatamone, 40, second floor. "A
     well-furnished room," he wrote in his diary, "sunshine for an hour or two
     in morning, just a glimpse of Somma," that is the north-east side of
     Vesuvius. The Strada Chiatamone runs parallel with the Via Partenope
     and with the quay from which one goes to the Castel dell'Ovo, which
     rises on a small rocky island, the Megaris of Pliny.

2   Gissing means the Riviera di Chiaia, celebrated before his day as a
     fashionable avenue, which runs along the gardens of the Villa Comunale
     (formerly the Villa Nazionale) on the sea-front.

3   A word much used at the time, which already appeared in the author's
     diary and correspondence on his first stay in Naples in November 1888.
     Old Naples was indeed vanishing.

4   The Pendino, in the eastern part of the town, was the most densely
     populated district of Naples. The Corso Umberto Primo, which was
     built across it from 1888 to 1894, made the way to the railway station
     and to the upper-class districts definitely easier.

5   Gissing's impressions of Naples are recorded in his diary, *London and the
     Life of Literature in Late Victorian England: The Diary of George Gissing,
     Novelist*, ed. Pierre Coustillas (Hassocks, Sussex: The Harvester Press,
     1978) and in *The Collected Letters of George Gissing*, ed. Paul F.
     Mattheisen, Arthur C. Young and Pierre Coustillas (Athens, Ohio: Ohio
     University Press, 1990-1997), Volumes III, IV, and VI.

6   In its modern form this oval-shaped fort was built under Don Pedro de
     Toledo, viceroy of Naples from 1532 to 1553. Access to it was by a
     bridge. In Gissing's time the castello was used as a military prison. Its
     main interest to him was cultural—the island of Megaris formed the
     centre of the Neapolitan villa of Lucullus, where Cicero met Brutus after
     the murder of Caesar in 44 BC.

7   Cab-drivers.

8   The Strada del Piliero skirts the Porto Grande, which was used for
     merchandise.

9   A village south-west of Naples, on the road to Pozzuoli. Gissing had
     recorded his impressions in a diary entry for 16 November 1888.

10   One of Gissing's favourite essayists (1605-1682), who wrote in *Religio
     Medici* (second part, ninth paragraph): "For even that vulgar and tavern

music, which makes one man merry, another mad, strikes in me a deep fit of devotion, and a profound contemplation of the first Composer, there is something in it of divinity more than the ear discovers."

11   A street renamed Via Roma in 1870. Originally it was named after the viceroy Don Pedro de Toledo. It led from the Piazza del Plebiscito to the Museum, a distance of about a mile and a half. In Gissing's time the old name continued to be used. The restaurant he had in mind was the Giardini di Torino, at no. 292. According to Baedeker, the establishment was famous for its cuisine and much frequented.

12   Clam soup.

13   Towns that were built on the shores of the Gulf of Taranto and of the Ionian Sea. Founded by Spartan Parthenians in 701 BC, Tarentum (Taras in Greek), nowadays Taranto, was once the most powerful city of Magna Græcia. Sybaris, nowadays Sibari, was founded in 720 BC by Achaeans and Troezenians and destroyed in 510 by the Crotonians. Croton, also founded in 720 BC, has remained famous on account of its most illustrious citizen, Pythagoras. Founded a little later, in 683 BC, Locri was extolled by Demosthenes for its wealth and love of art.

14   That is the Immacolatella Vecchia, where the offices of the customs house were situated. For an interesting comment on Gissing's "rather heavy portmanteau", see *With Gissing in Italy: The Memoirs of Brian Ború Dunne*, ed. Paul F. Mattheisen, Arthur C. Young and Pierre Coustillas (Athens, Ohio: Ohio University Press, 1999). Dunne, a young American who had met Gissing at Siena in the autumn of 1897 and saw him again in Rome before and after his journey to southern Italy, described him humorously leaving for Calabria "in his big overcoat and carrying an enormous valise, which really taxed the 'cabby' to load it into the hack... bound for the railway station. Gissing used to gloat over this canary-colored leather portable trunk—explaining that only the English knew how to tan leather" (p. 119).

15   Gissing had visited Greece in November and December 1889. See his *Diary* and Volume IV of the *Collected Letters*.

Chapter 2: Paola

1   Customs house.

2   The Albergo Leone was listed in Baedeker without comment. It stood in a small street off the Piazza del Popolo. The garden side of the house can be seen on two illustrations, on pp. 18 and 21 of *Città di Paola: Guida Turistica* (1989), and other views in the booklet suggest what Gissing could behold from the window of the Leone.

3   He means the Fontana Sette Canali.

4   These two dramatic episodes in the history of these parts are duly related by the French archaeologist, François Lenormant (1837-83) in his three-volume study, *La Grande-Grèce: Paysages et Histoire* (1881-84), which Gissing had read in the summer of 1897. Alaric I, the Goth (370-410), invaded Italy and, after besieging and ransacking Rome, ravaged the south of Italy and moved towards Sicily. He was taken ill on his way there and died at Consentia. See Gibbon's *Decline and Fall of the Roman Empire*, Vol. IV, p. 111 of the 1872 edition published by John Murray, as well as Lenormant, Vol. I, chapter 4, section 3, p. 229. Hannibal (247-182), the great Carthaginian general in the Second Punic War, had followed that route on his way back to Africa c. 210 BC.

CHAPTER 3: THE GRAVE OF ALARIC

1   Gissing means his edition of Murray's *Handbook for Travellers in Southern Italy and Sicily*, which declared that the Albergo dei Due Lionetti had a good trattoria. He very much regretted not having put up at the Albergo Vetere, near the public gardens by the theatre, which his Baedeker (1880 edition) recommended. If he had been able to consult Augustus Hare's *Cities of Southern Italy* (Smith, Elder, 1883), he would have been put off by its dismissive description: "Very miserable" (p. 341).

2   Besides his two guide books, he carried the three volumes of Lenormant's book.

3   There was notably the Excelsior, in the Corso Telesio, merely mentioned by Baedeker. Also the Hotel Rizzo, opposite the station, "very clean, and, for Southern Italy, very airy and comfortable" (Hare, p. 341).

4   At the end of his first year at Owens College, Gissing had been awarded as First Extra Junior Classical Prize an eight-volume leather bound copy of Gibbon's book in the new edition by William Smith, which included Notes by Dean Milman and Guizot, and is now in the editor's collection. The words "labour of a captive multitude" are Gibbon's, Vol. IV, p. 112, where the form Busentinus also appears.

5   Called "La libreria di Luigi Aprea".

6   *Don Quixote*, First Part, chapter 21.

7   That is, three leading figures in the fight for the unification of Italy.

8   Fourth Idyll, line 24. Lenormant also alludes to Theocritus about the Neaithos in the chapter he devotes to the valley of this river, Vol. I, ch. 8, section 1, as well as in his chapter on Cotrone and Pythagorean philosophy.

9   Renamed Teatro Alfonso Rendano to commemorate a famous local pianist and composer (1853-1931).

10   Gissing's assumption is highly plausible. Serious damage was done by
      earthquakes in 1783, 1854 and 1870. A new one was to happen in 1905.

11   The second tablet was replaced in 1944 by a new one commemorating
      the sacrifice of the martyrs who fell on 25 March 1844 when
      demonstrating for the unification of Italy.

12   Gibbon, *op. cit.*, Vol. IV, p. 112. Besides the comments and hypotheses
      of historians and archaeologists as to the site of Alaric's grave, one should
      note the ballad by the German Romantic poet Karl August von Platen-
      Hallermünde (1796-1835), "Das Grab im Busento", composed in 1820.

13   Zosimus, fifth-century author of an extant history in Greek of the
      Roman Empire up to about 410 AD. Gissing thought of this passage of
      Book V. 41 of *Historia Nova*: "Finally, since it was fated that everything
      having to do with the city's destruction should coincide, they not only
      stripped the images of their adornment but even melted down some of
      the gold and silver ones, among them that of Courage, whom the
      Romans call Virtus. With its destruction there was extinguished
      whatever courage and virtue the Romans had, just as it had been
      prophesied by men schooled in divination and ancestral ritual."
      (Translated by James J. Buchanan and Harold T. Davis, San Antonio,
      Texas: Trinity University Press, 1967, p. 239.)

CHAPTER 4: TARANTO

1   According to Gissing's diary, this man, who came from Genoa, was one
      Signor Questa.

2   See Chapter 2, note 4.

3   In *La Grande-Grèce*, Vol. I, chapter 5, section 8, Lenormant wrote : "On
      a narrow promontory off the hills of the Serra Pollinara, excavations
      conducted by Mr. Cavallari resulted in the discovery of the remains of a
      small temple which could not be entirely brought to light, but the
      terracotta antefixes of which unquestionably bear the hallmark of
      primitive art of the sixth century BC. It was a chapel erected by the
      Sybarites to one of their gods in the vicinity of their home town" (pp.
      326-27).

4   Gissing translates Lenormant rather freely. The phrase "incomparable
      beauty" is not in the original.

5   An echo from Lenormant who, on p. 226 of Volume I of *La Grande-
      Grèce*, compares the white oxen he has seen during his stays in Apulia
      with those reared by the Sybarites in ancient times.

6   Taranto was entirely destroyed by the Saracens in 927.

7   Gissing put up at the Albergo d'Europa in the Via Pitagora, an

establishment of good standing in the Borgo Nuovo, still extant today, with a view on the Mare Piccolo.

8   20 November was Saint Margaret's day. Queen Margherita (1851-1926), the wife of Umberto I, who reigned from 1878 to 1900.

9   The Cathedral of San Cataldo was founded in the eleventh century in what is now called the Old Town. Cataldo was a sixth-century monk who taught at Lismore, Ireland, after Saint Carthag's death. On his return from a pilgrimage to Jerusalem, he stopped at Tarentum and was appointed bishop of the town.

10   This triple evocation of characteristic moments in the history of Taranto ranges from the late fourth century BC to 927. Gissing first alludes to the time, after Socrates' death in 399 BC, when Plato visited the Pythagorians in Magna Græcia, then to the days of the Second Punic War, when the town espoused the cause of Hannibal, but was conquered in 209 by the Romans, who sold 30,000 of the citizens as slaves, lastly to the year 927, when the town was destroyed by the Saracens.

11   In *Cities of Southern Italy and Sicily* (Smith, Elder, 1883, p. 332) Augustus Hare wrote: "At the spot called Fontanella is the Monte di Chiocciole, a hill entirely formed of the shells (*Murex trunculus* and *Murex brandaris*) used in making the purple dye." See also Lenormant, *op. cit.*, Vol. I, chapter 1, section 11, p. 107, and before him Craufurd Tait Ramage, *The Nooks and By-Ways of Italy* (1868), chapter 20.

CHAPTER 5: DULCE GALÆSI FLUMEN

1   Horace, *Odes*, II, vi, 9-12.

2   The letter of introduction to the curator had been given to Gissing on 12 November 1897 by the British Consul in Naples, Eustace Neville-Rolfe (1854-1942), the author of *Naples in the Nineties* (1897). Gissing visited the museum on 21 November, and found the Director, Eduardo Caruso, "a jovial fellow, speaking English fairly well." Caruso told him entertaining anecdotes about the unconventional manners of the historian E. A. Freeman, whose daughter acted as a (sorely tried) interpreter, but he proved useless when it came to discussing local topography. Through the waiter at the hotel, Gissing heard of the existence of an English consul at Taranto, Wilfred Thesiger, whom he found "utterly ignorant of this country."

3   Most of these sketches were reproduced in the first and second English editions of *By the Ionian Sea* (Chapman and Hall, 1901 and 1905) as well as in the French translation of the book (Presses Universitaires du Septentrion, 1997). They are again reproduced in the present edition. Other sketches are still in the hands of Gissing's descendants.

4   This anecdote is related at greater length by Lenormant, *op. cit.*, Vol. I, chapter 1, section 5. There ensued war between Rome and Tarentum.

5   It is nothing new, and therefore of no interest.

6   Horace, *Odes*, II, vi, 13.

7   Gissing recorded the anecdote briefly in a diary entry for 20 November 1897: "The man at corner of streets, with picture of a miracle (10th Aug. 97) at the railway station near Loreto [province of Ancona]. Bought a copy of the story. Each time he mentioned a sacred name, he and crowd raised their hats." The swing-bridge was a few dozen yards away from the Albergo Europa.

8   To the great astonishment of all.

9   A rich gentleman.

10   Derogatory form of *frate*, mendicant friar.

11   *Nostro Signore Gesù Cristo*, Our Lord Jesus Christ.

CHAPTER 6: THE TABLE OF THE PALADINS

1   See note 4 to Chapter V.

2   As late as 1912 Baedeker's guide book declared that "a horse (2-3 fr.) may be ordered in advance from the 'Capostazione'" (station-master).

3   Here Gissing paraphrases Lenormant, *op. cit.*, Vol. I, chapter 2, section 2, p. 128.

4   This temple is generally said to have been dedicated to Hera, but Augustus Hare wrote that it was dedicated to Demeter (*op. cit.*, p. 337).

5   In the first English edition of the book, a full-page, black and white illustration shows the temple surrounded by this eyesore. The original was probably a postcard. In his book, published in 1883, Augustus Hare had responded to it much in the way Gissing did: "The ruins have lately been surrounded with a high wall by the Italian Government, so that all picturesque effect from the group of columns standing alone in the desolate country is destroyed ; and the dreary panorama, formerly visible from the temple itself, is completely shut out" (p. 337).

6   As his correspondence and diary testify, Gissing had visited Paestum in November 1888, during his first long stay in Italy.

7   What Gissing calls a little lake or a large pond was described in Murray's *Handbook* as a "small salt-water lagoon". It gradually silted up and was filled up in the twentieth century.

8   As Gissing observes, Pythagoras of Samos is reputed to have died in 497 BC at the age of ninety. He settled in Metapontum after being compelled to leave Croton, subsequently named Cotrone then Crotone, where he had established a "moral order" enforced by an élite of disciples who ruled over the town. According to various authorities, his grave was still

shown to visitors in the lifetime of Cicero, four hundred years later.

9   Unexpectedly yet strikingly, Gissing gives here the date of his journey to southern Italy.

10   Shakespeare, *Twelfth Night*, Act II, scene 2.

11   This proverb is either quoted or taken into account by many commentators who do not mention their sources, for instance Augustus Hare, *op. cit.*, p. 348. After many others, H. V. Morton wrote of the town of Crotone over thirty years ago: "It had the reputation of being the healthiest city of Magna Græcia; its athletes were always winning more than their share of prizes at the Olympic Games, and the reputation of its men, as well as of its women, for physical beauty may have had something to do with the course of training laid down by the Medical School, which at one time was considered the best not only in colonial Greece, but also in the Hellenic world. Herodotus has a lot to say about the School and tells us that the doctor of Darius, King of Persia, was Democedes of Croton. He was such a good doctor that the King kept him practically a prisoner in Persia, but being a Greek and full of subterfuge, he managed to escape." *A Traveller in Southern Italy* (London: Methuen, 1969), pp. 390-91.

12   Famous athlete who lived in the late sixth century BC and who led the army of Croton against Sybaris in 510. He gained six victories in wrestling at Olympia. Pausanias (VI, 14) relates some of his feats of strength.

13   Zeuxis of Heraclea, in southern Italy, a famous painter of ancient Greece (fifth century BC) celebrated for his success in rendering the beauty of female forms. He is best known for his picture of Helen for the temple of Hera mentioned by Gissing.

14   *La Divina Commedia*, Inferno, Canto I, 2: "Nel mezzo del cammín di nostra vita | Mi ritrovái per una selva oscura."

15   The city of Siris was founded by the Ionians of Colophon about the beginning of the seventh century BC on the banks of the river of that name, now called the Sinni, but the Sinno in Gissing's time. Hare (*op. cit.*, p. 339) explains that the city founded by the Ionians "rivalled Sybaris in its effeminacy and luxury, but, exciting the jealousy of the Achean colonies in the neighbourhood, was destroyed by them between 550 and 510 BC."

16   Lenormant, *op. cit.*, Vol. I, chapter 3, section 5.

CHAPTER 7: COTRONE

1   Palatial edifices with ground floors opening in arcades towards the street are one of the original architectural features of Bologna.

2   Once more we find Augustus Hare, whose book was published fourteen years before Gissing's, using a language which foreshadows that of his successor when relating his troubled days in this new halting-place. He describes the Albergo della Concordia as "very miserable", adding that "Cotrone is now so terribly unhealthy, that even one night spent there costs the lingerer an illness" (pp. 348-49). Contrastingly, in his 1912 edition, Baedeker declared the Concordia, which was situated on the Piazza Vittoria, to be "well spoken of", an admittedly improved reputation confirmed by Norman Douglas in his chapter "Memories of Gissing" in *Old Calabria* (1915).

3   Many photographs of the Albergo Concordia, now Italia, have been published in Italian reviews and newspapers. Recent examples of old postcards beautifully reproduced can be found in Virgilio Squillace's article, "L'Albergo di Douglas, Gissing e Lenormant," *Calabria*, August 2001, pp. 58-81 and in the more recent one by Luigi Abbramo, "Italia Nostra per il 'Concordia' : L'attuale 'Italia' ospitò Gissing, Douglas e Lenormant," *Gazzetta del Sud*, 6 April 2002, p. 26.

4   Augustus Hare thought the Albergo Minerva "quite wretched" (p. 348).

5   Gissing's hostess was Signora Filomena Fedele, born in 1853. She had died by the time Norman Douglas visited Cotrone in the next decade. Of her son, whom Gissing describes as his "chambermaid ... a lively little fellow of about twelve years old" in Chapter 10, Douglas has nothing to say and nothing is known of him. It should be noted that in his diary for 1 December 1897, Gissing speaks of his "chambermaid" as a "little imp of a lad (about 10 yrs old)."

6   In the early sixteenth century.

7   Gissing's descendants still own these field glasses, which were on show at the Gissing exhibition organized by the National Book League in June 1971. See John Spiers and Pierre Coustillas, *The Rediscovery of George Gissing* (London, 1971), p. 136.

8   "Heaven's thought was otherwise," Virgil, *Aeneid*, II, 428.

9   Gissing repeats here the information supplied by Lenormant: "According to Nola-Molisi [1649], the temple was still almost undamaged with its forty-eight columns standing in the early sixteenth century, and it was then only that bishop Antonio Lucifero [1510-1521] had it pulled down and used the materials for the reconstruction of the bishop's palace in Cotrone." *Op. cit.*, Vol. II, chapter 11, section 2. The legitimate indignation of Lenormant, who refers to the affair as "episcopal vandalism", is echoed in Gissing's correspondence during his stay at Cotrone from 25 November to 6 December 1897. See his letters to his publisher A. H. Bullen and to his friend Edward Clodd of 27 November. He used such phrases as "ecclesiastical ruffian" and "ecclesiastical scoundrel".

10   Notably by Augustus Hare, *op. cit.*, p. 349.

11   *La Grande-Grèce*, Vol. II, chapter 10, sections 10 and 11, *passim.*

12   This uncongenial local grandee, Marchese Anselmo Berlingieri (1852-1911) was mayor of Cotrone from 1896 to 1899. (Like Augustus Hare and others, Gissing misspelt Berlingieri's name.) That the ill-educated, condescending *sindaco* was a wealthy landowner is confirmed by a footnote in the Italian translation of Lenormant's book (1976 edition, p. 184, note 36). In his introduction Armando Lucifero makes it clear that the orchards belonged to Marquis Berlingieri.

13   The long row of warehouses and some of the big padlocks are still visible to this day.

14   Leigh Hunt (1784-1859), *The Story of Rimini* (1816), line 430.

CHAPTER 8: FACES BY THE WAY

1   As an example of this, see the interesting entry for 29 November 1889 in Gissing's diary.

2   This was Giulio Marino, born in 1843 or 1844, who died at Cotrone on 9 February 1901. His encounter with Gissing was a landmark in his life and it has been remembered by the next four generations. Marino was, as Gissing noted in his diary as well as in his book, a distinguished man with cultural aspirations. See Teresa Liguori, "Una bella amicizia," *La Provincia KR*, 21 July 2001, p. 13, and Teresa Liguori and Pierre Coustillas, "'At Cemetery found a delightful guardian': The Crotone Gardener Identified," *Gissing Journal*, October 2001, pp. 1-6. Of Marino's culture evidence has been produced by his great-grandson, Domenico Marino, an archæologist, who holds books by Darwin and Thomas Moore (in Italian translation) and Giuseppe Giusti, which once belonged to his ancestor (see Pierre Coustillas, "Gissing and Calabria," *Gissing Journal*, October 2002, pp. 26-27). In *Old Calabria* Norman Douglas refers feelingly to Marino's death and to his "poor little grave" in his chapter "Memories of Gissing".

3   The gentleman was Baron Luigi Berlingieri (1816-1900), and Giulio Marino accompanied him in his many journeys in Italy and abroad, notably in England, France, Austria and Switzerland.

4   Lenormant, who knew Marquis Antonio Lucifero personally, throws useful light on the Lucifero family. See *La Grande-Grèce*, Vol. II, chapter II, section 10, in which it appears that the Luciferos have become liberals and republicans. It is appropriate to add that the Italian translation of the three volumes, which was first published in 1935, was the work of Antonio Lucifero's son Armando (1855-1933), whose own son Falcone contributed a preface to the 1976 edition.

5   See the entry for 13 December 1889 in Gissing's diary.

6   Giulio Marino died about four months before *By the Ionian Sea* was published in book form, but materially there would have been just a possibility for him to hear before he did that Gissing had described their meeting in well-chosen terms in the serial version of his narrative, which appeared in the *Fortnightly Review* on 1 July 1900. Indeed he could have read in the Catanzaro weekly, *La Giostra*, for 29 October 1900, the notoriously mistaken comments passed by the editor on the chapters devoted to Catanzaro, the town visited by Gissing after he left Cotrone.

7   On this little church, see Norman Douglas's comments in chapter 36 of *Old Calabria.*

CHAPTER 9: MY FRIEND THE DOCTOR

1   In *Notes and Queries* for 18 February 1950 ("Borgian Cheese", p. 80) an Italian living in Rome, Augusto Guidi, pointed out that Gissing was mistaken about *cacio cavallo.* "Actually," he wrote, "the butter concerned is 'part' of the cheese, the very core of it, left fused in order to improve its taste and flavour: the cheese in question is much valued and held a sort of 'dainty' in South Italy."

2   Riccardo Sculco (1855-1931) had been a student in the University of Naples, where he graduated in 1884. He became a municipal councillor, then in 1891-92 mayor of Cotrone. He is commemorated with Gissing, Lenormant and Douglas on the plaque which was put up at the entrance of the former Albergo Concordia on 22 June 2002.

3   Apparently Alfredo Zurlo (1887-1966). Norman Douglas wrote in his "Memories of Gissing" (*Old Calabria*) that "the little waiter is alive and now married." He referred to the years 1907-1911.

4   He was awaiting among other things the typescript of his critical study of Dickens's works, a book which was published in London by Blackie and Son on 15 February 1898. His diary gives details about the "great heap of letters" he found at the Catanzaro post-office on his arrival on 7 December. Vol. VII of his *Collected Letters* contains seven of the letters and postcards he sent during the next couple of days.

5   According to Georges and Huguette Vallet in *Naples et l'Italie du Sud* (Paris: Presses Universitaires de France, 1966, p. 236), Hannibal left in the Temple of Hera, "on bronze tables, in Greek and Carthaginian, the story of his high deeds in Italy, before he ordered to be massacred near the temple all the Italian mercenaries who refused to follow him."

CHAPTER 10: CHILDREN OF THE SOIL

1   The housemaid, "the domestic serf with dark and fiercely flashing eyes," Norman Douglas says, was also dead by the time of his first visit.

2   So as to convey something of the local colour, Gissing uses a number of Italian words and phrases: *guai*, plural form of *guaio*: woes, troubles; *tanto lavorato*: worked so much; *un po' di calma*: calm down; quiet, please; *pessimo tempo*: bad weather; *grazie a voi, Signore*: my thanks to you, sir.

CHAPTER 11: THE MOUNT OF REFUGE

1   Dangerous, extremely dangerous.

2   How much Gissing paid on leaving the Albergo Concordia is unknown, but Dr. Sculco's agenda for 1897 has survived. He was called upon to visit Gissing twice a day from 28 November to 2 December, once on the 3rd and again once on the 4th. His fee amounted to 24 lire. See Francesco Badolato, "Meeting Dr. Sculco's Son," *Gissing Newsletter*, July 1974, pp. 7-8, and Gissing's diary for late November and early December 1897. In chapter 36 of *Old Calabria* Norman Douglas relates his visit to Dr. Sculco in 1907 or shortly afterwards: "I called on this gentleman, hoping to obtain from him some reminiscences of Gissing, whom he attended during a serious illness. 'Yes,' he replied, to my enquiries, 'I remember him quite well; the young English poet who was ill here. I prescribed for him. Yes—yes ! He wore his hair long.' And that was all I could draw from him. I have noticed more than once that Italian physicians have a stern conception of the Hippocratic oath: the affairs of their patients, dead or alive, are a sacred trust in perpetuity." H. V. Morton echoed this anecdote, *op. cit.*, p. 392.

CHAPTER 12: CATANZARO

1   Quick.

2   Gissing put up at the Albergo Centrale, on the Corso Vittorio Emanuele (today Corso Mazzini), which Baedeker declared to be "well spoken of ".

3   In 1783. The earthquake of 1832 was also a cause of serious injury, as was to be, after Gissing's death, that of September 1905.

4   Built in 1060 by Robert Guiscard (1015-1085), founder of the Norman settlements in southern Italy, and destroyed in the late 1870s, as is confirmed by Lenormant, "so as to facilitate access to the town and to

enable it to develop freely on the only side where it is not bordered with precipices." But the French historian feared that political passion may have accounted as much as the necessities of town-planning for the pulling down of this mediaeval castle. *Op. cit.*, Vol. II, chapter 13, section 1, p. 276.

5   Nicephorus II Phocas (c. 913-969), Emperor from 963 to his death. He was assassinated by John I Tzimiskes, who was his successor until 976.

6   Baron Pasquale Cricelli, a wealthy landowner, was English Vice-Consul at Catanzaro from 27 March 1893 to 29 February 1904, when the post was abolished. He succeeded his father Alphonso Cricelli, who had been appointed on 11 December 1851. For Gissing's cicerone, see the author's diary for 6-10 December 1897.

7   The two following anecdotes are borrowed from *La Grande-Grèce*, Vol. II, chapter 13, section 3, and H. V. Morton in turn relates how generously Gissing was welcomed in Catanzaro. *Op. cit.*, p. 389. He it is who called "bill snatchers" those dinner guests in southern Italy, Catanzaresi in particular, who secretly arrange with the manager to pay the bill.

8   This pharmacy, known at the time as the Farmacia Leone (now Farmacia Tambato) is indeed a curiosity, easily noticeable on the ground floor of the Palazzo Fazzari in the Corso Mazzini (formerly Corso Vittorio Emanuele). Its originality has often been celebrated, in illustrated books as in histories of the town, where photographs of the outside, with its arresting sign (*mostra*), and of the inside, with its stupendous furniture and decoration, can be seen. The shop stands practically opposite what used to be the Albergo Centrale, and still preserves fittings described by Gissing. It was founded in 1841 by Dr. Federico Leone, who was succeeded by his nephews Nicola and Alfonso Leone. See in particular Beppe Mazzocca and Antonio Panzarella, *Cara Catanzaro* (Soveria Mannelli: Rubbettino Editore, 1987) and Sergio Dragone, *Catanzaro: I luoghi, le persone, la storia* (Catanzaro: Cinesud due Editore, 1996, 4 vols.).

9   Where Gissing had stayed from 25 September to 8 November 1897, writing *Charles Dickens, a Critical Study*, before starting on his journey by the Ionian Sea.

10   Gissing's sources for these two stories are obscure. Lenormant only mentions the former. Historians now agree that Catanzaro was founded in the tenth century by the Byzantines. The Turkish invasion of Greece took place in the second half of the fifteenth century.

CHAPTER 13: THE BREEZY HEIGHT

1   On the manuscript the title was at first "The Windy Height".

2   The Museo Civico stands on the left-hand side as one enters the Villa
     Trieste. It was formally opened in 1895. At the time of Gissing's visit the
     director was Oreste Dito (1866-1934), who gave him a copy of the
     Transactions of the Accademia di Catanzaro containing an article about
     Cassiodorus. It proved useful in due course.

3   Practically nothing is known of this man, except that he died locally. He
     had been a widower for twenty-five years at the time of Gissing's visit,
     his wife having died in childbirth in 1872. He is buried, without any
     indication of his life dates, in the mortuary chapel of the Figliolo family
     to be found in the local cemetery. His name became an international
     word, mainly in its plural form *paparazzi*, when the film director
     Federico Fellini and his friend Ennio Flaiano, trying to find a suitable
     name for the memorable press photographer in *La dolce vita*, happened
     upon that of Coriolano Paparazzo in the recently published Italian
     translation of *By the Ionian Sea* by the poet Margherita Guidacci
     (Cappelli, 1957). In Italy *paparazzo/i* promptly became a neologism and
     was duly recorded in dictionaries, but it was not until it was abruptly
     used on a worldwide scale after Princess Diana's dramatic death in late
     August 1997 that the word became a common one in most languages.
     The literature on the subject is abundant. See in particular, Francesco
     Badolato and Pierre Coustillas, "Gissing and the Paparazzi," *Gissing
     Journal*, October 1997, pp. 29-35, and "More on Gissing and the
     Paparazzi," January 1998, pp. 19-22. A plaque commemorating
     Gissing's stay at the Albergo Centrale was unveiled on the front of the
     former albergo on 23 October 1999. See P. Coustillas, D. Grylls, B.
     Postmus, "Gissing in Catanzaro: A Commemoration," *Gissing Journal*,
     January 2000, pp. 11-25. The proceedings of the symposium held on
     the occasion, copiously illustrated, were published by Mauro F.
     Minervino, *George Gissing at Catanzaro*, Catanzaro: Biblioteca
     comunale [2002].

4   Not the main theatre in the town, which was the Teatro Comunale,
     founded in 1830 and pulled down in March 1938.

5   Chapters 13 to 15 of *By the Ionian Sea*, which were serialized in the 1
     September 1900 number of the *Fortnightly Review*, were brought to the
     notice of the editor of the Catanzaro weekly *La Giostra*, who, on the
     front page of the number for 29 October 1900, passed obtuse comment
     on the end of Chapter 13, which he largely misunderstood. There is no
     evidence that Gissing ever became aware of this early Italian response to
     his work, entitled "Catanzaro giudicata da un giornalista inglese ". For

the English translation of this leader, see Pierre Coustillas, "'Catanzaro Judged by an English Journalist,'" *Gissing Journal*, July 2000, pp. 22-26.

CHAPTER 14: SQUILLACE

1   Virgil, *Aeneid*, III, 553.

2   The last Roman consul (c. 490-585), who was also a quæstor, prefect and historian. He was a minister under Odoacer, Theodoric, Amalasontha and Athalaric. He preserved his office under Theodatus and Vitigis. At the age of seventy he decided to pass the rest of his life in religious solitude and founded at Scylacium, in Bruttium, two monasteries (Monasterium Vivariense and Castellense) on the site of his father's villa, where he himself was born. He assumed the direction of Vivariense but declined to take the rank of abbot. Neither Belisarius, who represented Byzantine power, nor Totila, king of the Ostrogoths, violated his haven of peace.

3   Partly for health reasons, Gissing lived at Budleigh Salterton from February to May 1897. In a letter to his German friend Eduard Bertz, dated 16 April 1897, he also gives details about the edition of the works of Cassiodorus he was reading with great pleasure: *Opera Omnia*, two volumes, folio, published in Venice in 1729.

4   Beastly weather!

5   Mons Moscius is mentioned by Cassiodorus in his *Variæ*, Book XII, 15, 4; he had his two monasteries built on that mount, nowadays called Coscia di Stalletti, as Gissing notes further on.

6   Neither Baedeker nor Murray mentioned this albergo. The building, with a storey added to it, still stands and is numbered 37 in what is now Via Damiano Assanti. The old inn was recently a *studio legale* which had closed down.

CHAPTER 15: MISERIA

1   Gissing heard this remark on 15 December 1897 at the Villa Mario Varrone, Cassino, the small town at the foot of Monte Cassino (diary). He was on his way back to Rome after his journey in the far South.

2   The monastery of Santa Chiara dates back to the early seventeenth century. It was largely destroyed by the earthquake of 1783. Only its front is still standing.

3   Built about 1044 by the Norman Guillaume de Hauteville on the site of a Byzantine fortress. It has been restored in recent years.

4   Lenormant sums up the two opinions as follows: "For some scholars such as Barrio, Marafioti, Fiore, M. Mazocchi and M. Marincola-Pistoja,

modern Squillace stands exactly where ancient Scylaceum used to be. For others the antique town was by the seaside and its population moved inland, to the height of Squillace, in the days of Saracen incursions. Lupis and Alberti think they have discovered the remains of Scylaceum on the north-west side of the Stalletti promontory." *Op. cit.*, Vol. II, chapter 14, section 5.

5   Lenormant translates at length a passage from *Variae*, XII, 15, which we reproduce in S. J. B. Barnish's English version: "That city is sited on the Adriatic gulf [Cassiodorus should have written the Ionian Sea], and hangs from the hillside like a bunch of grapes, not that it may swell with pride in the difficulty of its ascent, but that it may gaze with delight on green meadows, and the blue back of the sea. It watches the sun's birth in its very cradle, where the coming day sends no light of dawn before it, but straightway, as it begins to rise, the flashing rays reveal its torch. It gazes on the joys of Phoebus, and so shines there with its own pure radiance that you would think it his true country, and the fame of Rhodes surpassed" (*Cassiodorus: Variae*, translated with notes and introduction by S. J. B. Barnish, Liverpool University Press, 1992, pp. 169-70).

6   The third (posthumously published) volume of *La Grande-Grèce* (1884) contains a preface by the author in which he sketches what his gigantic enquiry into the past and present of southern Italy was to consist of. Unfortunately he died on 9 December 1883, before his third volume was quite completed and with the fourth volume only planned.

7   Gissing sent the bill to Baron Pasquale Cricelli on 29 December 1897, shortly after his return to Rome.

8   Gissing means Murray's and Baedeker's guide books. In his 1892 edition the former described the town as "placed on an almost inaccessible rock, 5 miles distant, and invisible from the station" (p. 269). The 1912 edition of Baedeker still declared that we only "catch a glimpse of it (right) as we approach" (p. 271).

CHAPTER 16: CASSIODORUS

1   See *Variae*, Book XII, 15.

2   *Ibid.*, I, 4, 14.

3   On Cassiodorus and his ancestors, see Lenormant, *op. cit.*, Vol. II, chapter 14, sections 1 to 6, and S. J. B. Barnish, *op. cit.*, pp. xxxv-liii.

4   According to Lenormant, Cassiodorus was born c. 469 or 470. Gissing preferred to follow Baedeker. Boethius (Anicius Manlius Severinus Boethius), author of the *Consolation of Philosophy*, lived from c. 480 to

524; Benedict of Nursia, called St. Benedict, from c. 480 to 547. He founded the monastery at Monte Cassino about 529.

5   Theodoric (c. 454-526), King of the Ostrogoths from c. 474 to his death. The capital of his kingdom, which extended across Italy and the Dalmatian shore, was Ravenna, to the history of which Gissing devoted a long narrative poem when he was a student at Owens College, Manchester.

6   Which he wrote between 518 and 521 by order of Theodoric. Divided into twelve books, it described their origins, their habitat and their character.

7   That is until 542. See the list of Ostrogothic sovereigns in note 2 to Chapter 14.

8   Namely between the capital of the Western Empire (under Honorius, in 402), which was by then the capital of the Ostrogothic kingdom, and the capital of the Eastern Empire.

9   This quotation appears in Gissing's notes on Cassiodorus held by the Lilly Library, Indiana University. Gissing does not give its source, *Variae*, Book II, 27. The translation of this quotation is also given by Gissing in chapter 13 of his unfinished historical novel of Roman and Goth, set in sixth-century Rome, *Veranilda*.

10 For a thematic list of Cassiodorus' digressions, see S. J. B. Barnish's edition, pp. 199-200.

11 Cassiodorus, *Institutiones*, Liber Primus, XXX, 1. In these last few paragraphs of Chapter 16, whether he quotes in Latin or in English, or merely paraphrases, Gissing's comment is based on Liber Primus, XXVIII to XXXII.

12 *Psalms*, CXXVIII, 2.

13 Matthew, XI, 30.

14 For Denys the Little or Exiguus, see Gissing's main source, Lenormant, *op. cit.*, Vol. II, chapter 14, section 4. He was a learned monk of the sixth century with an enviable knowledge of Greek and Latin, also an accomplished mathematician and astronomer. His name, however, is chiefly remembered as that of the man who introduced the method of reckoning the dates of the Christian era that we now use.

15 Here, too, Gissing borrows from the same section in Lenormant. Led by Alboin, the Lombards invaded the north of Italy about the time of Cassiodorus' death. They ransacked Roman Catholic churches and convents.

Chapter 17: The Grotta

1   *La Grande-Grèce*, Vol. II, chapter 14, section 5.

2   Gissing's Note: There is debate among scholars whether the name should be Cassiodorus or Cassiodorius. We have rhythmic authority for the common spelling, which is euphonically preferable; but German erudition pronounces for the *-ius*. These fellow-countrymen of the sage called him unmistakably Cassiodorio. The local nomenclature can hardly have any historic significance; it is probably quite modern.

3   The Fontana di Cassiodoro is mentioned by Augustus Hare, *op. cit.*, p. 352.

4   The Monasterium Vivariense founded by Cassiodorus was succeeded, on the same site, by the monastery of Stallacti dedicated to St. Gregory the Thaumaturgist (c. 213-c. 270), a theologian of the Eastern Church and bishop of Caesarea.

5   Porter.

6   The schoolboy and Gissing had passed Montauro and Soverato before arriving at San Sostene. Young De Luca's card was preserved by Gissing. It is now in the editor's collection.

7   The priest of San Nicolà at Badolato was Don Giuseppe Minniti, who had been ordained by the bishop of Squillace in 1864 at the age of twenty-two or twenty-three. He remained the parish priest until his death in August 1924.

Chapter 18: Reggio

1   The history of Reggio Calabria is indeed an unquiet one. Known as Rhegium in antiquity, the town was captured and destroyed in 387 BC by Dionysius I of Syracuse, then in 270 BC by the Romans. In the Middle Ages the town passed into the hands of Totila, King of the Ostrogoths, in 549, was conquered by the Saracens in 918, by the Pisans in 1005, by Robert Guiscard in 1060, and later by the Turks on several occasions, especially in 1552 and 1597.

2   The earthquake of 1783 killed about 30,000 people, and that of 1908 was again to destroy the most part of the city.

3   This castle, the south side of which dates back to the fifteenth century, somehow resisted the shock of the earthquake of 1908.

4   Gissing's diary shows that he put up at the Albergo Sicilia.

5   The young soldier was Emilio Cuzzocrea, who fell in the early morning of 21 August 1860 near the castle during the battle for the liberation of the city. He was twenty years old. A street of Reggio bears his name. After

this quotation Gissing cancelled a fourteen-line passage in his microscopic hand on the manuscript. It was a paragraph in strong criticism of British indifference to the sufferings of foreign peoples. He very likely came to think that it spoilt the structure of the final chapter. Jacob Korg transcribed it in his article "An Unpublished Passage of *By the Ionian Sea*," *Gissing Newsletter,* July 1984, pp. 26-28.

6   John Pemble has stressed the remarkable prescience of this passage in which Gissing "foretold that the patriotic idealism of the Risorgimento would be betrayed and that Italy herself would become a blood-stained oppressor" (*The Mediterranean Passion,* p. 239).

7   XXVIII, 13. Only the outer walls and two storeys of the right tower escaped destruction during the earthquake of 1908. When the cathedral was rebuilt, the inscription that used to be carved in Latin across the front was carved again, in Greek, over the portal.

8   "I will build my church." This is part of the inscription on the frieze running round the inside of the dome at St. Peter's.

9   The Museo Civico of Reggio was formally opened in 1882. If one considers his allusion to the "sixteen years of life" he had spent in the museum and D. Coppola's report on the activities in the field of antiquities and the fine arts in Calabria Ulteriore from 1840 to 1916, it is obvious that the director in late 1897 was Giuseppe Vazzana. In 1893 he established a very useful archaeological map of Reggio Calabria in the nineteenth century. His career ended under a cloud. In 1901 he was involved in a major scandal about the theft of ancient gold coins that had been given to the museum. Although he was declared free of blame in 1903, the affair has remained unclear in some respects. *Klearchos,* XXIV, 1982, nos. 93-96, pp. 13-93.

10   Gissing described at some length his visit to the museum in his diary (12 December 1897).

11   The first two volumes of a set of twelve in Latin. Publication, under the general editorship of the German philologist and historian Theodor Mommsen (1817-1903), had begun in 1862.

12   The painter was Giuseppe Benassai (1835-1878), a Reggio artist who studied painting under Fergola in Naples and exhibited his works in that town in 1859, in Milan in 1865, and in Paris two years later. The two paintings mentioned by Gissing were "Aspromonte" (1869) and "La Quiete" (1868). They can be seen in the museum, restyled Museo Nazionale.

13   The visitors' book did not perish in 1908. Lenormant's signature and that of Gissing ("George Gissing. Londra. 12/12/97") were reproduced in facsimile in "George Gissing (1857-1903)" by Ernesta and Albert Spencer Mills, *Calabria Sconosciuta,* April-June 1980, pp. 24-27.

14   The Via Agostino Plutino was the south end of the Via Marina, on the
      seafront. For images of Reggio before the earthquake of 28 December
      1908, see Agazio Trombetta, *Saluti da Reggio Calabria* (Reggio:
      Corpododici Edizioni, 1993).

FURTHER READING

I George Gissing's Works

Most of Gissing's major works are mentioned in the Introduction. Only three novels should be added: *Denzil Quarrier* (1892), which in some respects foreshadows the main theme of *The Odd Women*; *The Crown of Life* (1899), a love story set against an anti-imperialist background; and *Will Warburton*, subtitled *A Romance of Real Life* (1905). His short stories were collected in *Human Odds and Ends* (1898), *The House of Cobwebs* (1906), *A Victim of Circumstances* (1927), *Short Stories of To-day and Yesterday* (1929), which is a selection from the three previous volumes, *Stories and Sketches* (1938). The early tales of the American period were collected in *The Sins of the Fathers* (1924, ed. Vincent Starrett), *Brownie* (1931, ed. George Everett Hastings *et al*), and *George Gissing: Lost Stories from America* (1992, ed. Robert L. Selig). Other early works have been published: *An Heiress on Condition* (1923), *George Gissing: Essays and Fiction* (1970), *My First Rehearsal and My Clerical Rival* (1970), the last two edited by Pierre Coustillas, who also published *A Freak of Nature or Mr. Brogden, City Clerk* (1990) and *The Day of Silence* (1993). Gissing's verse was collected by Bouwe Postmus under the title *The Poetry of George Gissing* (1995).

Two important sources of information for *By the Ionian Sea* and Gissing's interest in the world of classical antiquity are: *London and the Life of Literature in Late Victorian England: The Diary of George Gissing, Novelist*, ed. Pierre Coustillas (1978) and *The Collected Letters of George Gissing*, ed. Paul Mattheisen *et al*, 9 vols. (1990-97).

II *By the Ionian Sea*

The first edition was published in June 1901 by Chapman and Hall, with illustrations in colour by the Austrian artist Leo de Littrow and others in black and white based on sketches by Gissing and other material supplied by him. The same publishers reprinted the book with the black and white illustrations only in March and June 1905, then in 1917 and 1921. In 1933 Jonathan Cape included the volume, preceded by an essay on Gissing by Virginia Woolf, in his Traveller's Library. New editions were published in 1956 (Richards Press), 1961 (Icon Books), 1963 (John Baker), 1986 (Century Hutchinson), and 1992 (Tragara Press, limited edition). A Colonial edition was brought out by T. Fisher Unwin in 1905.

In the United States the following editions were published: 1905 and 1917 (Scribner), 1920 (Mosher), 1933 (Harrison Smith), 1963 (Dufour), 1991 (Marlboro Press), 1996 (Marlboro/Northwestern University).

In Italy a translation by Margherita Guidacci appeared under the imprint of Cappelli in 1957. It was reprinted in 1962 and 1971. The Edizioni di Torino published a slightly revised version of it, supplemented by critical material and edited by Francesco Mauro Minervino, in 1993. Paola M. Reale edited an abridged version of the English text for Edizioni Parallelo 38 of Naples in 1980.

In France an illustrated critical edition of a translation by Hélène and Pierre Coustillas was published by the Presses Universitaires du Septentrion in 1997.

In Japan an annotated and illustrated translation by Tadashi Sasaki came out under the imprint of Shingetsu-sha in 1947. The notes to this edition were pioneering work. A new annotated translation by Shigeru Koike was published by Shûbun International in 1988. A revised edition of this, with illustrations and an afterword, was published by Iwanami Shoten in 1994. An abridged, annotated Japanese edition in English by U. Miyagi (Sekkei-Syobo, 1958) has been frequently reprinted; so has another by Chiyokichi Tsuda (Shohakusha, 1970).

A German translation by Karina Of, with a foreword by Pierre Coustillas and an afterword by Wulfhard Stahl, appeared in early 2003 (Wiborada Verlag).

III Biographies, Correspondence and Critical Studies

The only reliable, though partly superseded, biography is *George Gissing: A Critical Biography*, by Jacob Korg (1963, revised editions 1965 and 1980), but at least two works, *The Born Exile: George Gissing*, by Gillian Tindall (1974) and *Gissing: A Life in Books*, by John Halperin (1982 and 1987), which discuss the relationship between the author and his works, are devoted to important aspects of the life.

Many volumes of letters to a variety of correspondents were published from 1914 to 1987, but except for the critical apparatus of the best of them they are superseded. See above.

The most significant critical studies are *Gissing in Context* (1975), by Adrian Poole; *George Gissing, Ideology and Fiction* (1978), by John Goode; *George Gissing* (1983, revised edition 1995), by Robert L. Selig; *The Paradox of Gissing* (1986), by David Grylls; *George Gissing: The Cultural Challenge* (1989), by John Sloan ; and *"The Vice of Wedlock": The Theme of Marriage in George Gissing's Novels* (1994), by Christina Sjöholm.

Of special interest to readers of *By the Ionian Sea* will be Samuel Vogt Gapp's dated, yet useful, specialized study, *George Gissing, Classicist* (1936, reprinted 1972 and 1977).

IV *By the Ionian Sea* and the Critics

A selection of reviews of the first two editions, published in 1901 and 1905, as well as a list of additional reviews, will be found in *Gissing: The Critical Heritage*, ed. Pierre Coustillas and Colin Partridge (1972, reprinted 1985 and 1995). Two articles by Mario Praz and Gabriele Armandi on *By the Ionian Sea* (see below) were reprinted in *George Gissing: Antologia Critica*, ed. Francesco Badolato (Rome: Herder, 1984). The same editor published with comments a translation of the Italian portions of Gissing's diary under the title *Da Venezia allo Stretto di Messina* (Rome: Herder, 1989).

The following assessments in English appeared for the most part in the English and American press. Few of them have been reprinted.

E. A. Bennett, "A Gossip about Books," *Hearth and Home*, 4 July 1901, p. 374.

Anon., "The Plain Dealer in Southern Italy," *St. James's Gazette*, 11 July 1901, p. 12.

Anon., "Review of Books: By the Ionian Sea," *Times Weekly Edition Supplement*, 19 July 1901, p. iii.

W. Somerset Maugham, "Our Book of the Week: *By the Ionian Sea*," *Sunday Sun*, 11 August 1901, p. 1. Reprinted in *A Traveller in Romance*, by the same author (1984).

[Edith Lister], "Some Recollections of George Gissing," *Gentleman's Magazine*, February 1906, pp. 11-18.

J[ames] C[uthbert] H[adden], "Readers and Writers," *Wolverhampton Chronicle*, 20 January 1909, p. 2.

Anon., "Books Worth Reading: *By the Ionian Sea*," *New York Times Book Review*, 2 December 1917, p. 328.

T. Earle Welby, "Escape from Grub Street—George Gissing," in *Second Impressions* (London, 1933).

A. R. Orage, "Gissing's Malady," in *Selected Essays and Critical Writings* (London, 1935).

Michael Lloyd, "Italy and the Nostalgia of George Gissing," *English Miscellany*, no. 2, 1951, pp. 171-98.

Patrick Leigh Fermor, "From Murk to Sunlight," *Sunday Times*, 3 February 1957, p. 6.

R. R., "Book Supplement," *Twentieth Century*, May 1957, pp. 507-08.

B. P. Agelasto, "Some English Travellers in Italy," *Books* (The Journal of the National Book League), May-June 1963, pp. 105-09.

H. V. Morton, *A Traveller in Southern Italy* (London, 1969). *Passim.*

P. F. Kirby, "Norman Douglas, Gissing and Lenormant in South Italy," in *Critical Dimensions*, ed. Mario Curreli and Alberto Martino (Cuneo, 1978).

Francesco Badolato, "The Influence of Virgil on George Gissing," *Helikon*, XX-XXI (1980-81), pp. 411-16.

Jacob Korg, "An Unpublished Passage of *By the Ionian Sea*," *Gissing Newsletter*, July 1984, pp. 26-28.

John Pemble, *The Mediterranean Passion: Victorian and Edwardian Travellers in the South* (Oxford, 1987). *Passim.*

Manfred Pfister (ed.), *The Fatal Gift of Beauty: The Italies of British Travellers, An Annotated Anthology* (Amsterdam, 1996).

I. C., "Travel," *Times Literary Supplement*, 2 May 1997, p. 32.

Pierre Coustillas, "The First Paparazzo," *Times Literary Supplement*, 12 September 1997, p. 17.

Francesco Badolato and Pierre Coustillas, "Gissing and the Paparazzi," *Gissing Journal*, October 1997, pp. 29-35. Also by the same authors, "More about Gissing and the Paparazzi," January 1998, pp. 19-22.

Martin Garrett, *Traveller's Literary Companion to Italy* (Brighton, 1998).

Paul F. Mattheisen, Arthur C. Young and Pierre Coustillas (eds.), *With*

Gissing in Italy: The Memoirs of Brian Ború Dunne (Athens, Ohio, 1999).

Pierre Coustillas, "Revisiting the Shores of the Ionian Sea," *Gissing Journal* (Supplement), October 1999, pp. 6-43.

Pierre Coustillas, David Grylls and Bouwe Postmus, "Gissing in Catanzaro: A Commemoration," *Gissing Journal*, January 2000, pp. 11-25.

Teresa Liguori and Pierre Coustillas, "'At Cemetery found a delightful guardian': The Crotone Gardener Identified," *Gissing Journal*, October 2001, pp. 1-6.

Allan W. Atlas, "George Gissing on Music: Italian Impressions," *Gissing Journal*, January 2002, pp. 1-24.

Italian publications of Gissing interest in Italy, especially in the deep South, have been numerous since the 1960s. The following is a selection of volumes and articles which appeared in journals and newspapers.

Anon., "Catanzaro giudicata da un giornalista inglese," *La Giostra* (Catanzaro), 29 October 1900, p. 1. Translated in the *Gissing Journal*, July 2000, pp. 22-26.

Pietro De-Logu, "La Calabria: Vista da uno scrittore inglese; George Gissing in viaggio da Paola a Cosenza," *Il Ponte*, September-October 1950, pp. 1326-27.

Giacomo Antonini, "Il ritorno di George Gissing," *La Fiera letteraria*, 10 November 1957, p. 4.

Br., "Da Swinburne a Gissing," *Brutium*, May-June 1958, pp. 1-3.

Mario Praz, "Gita alla colonna," *Il Tempo*, 19 July 1958, p. 3.

Piero Mandrillo, "Un scrittore inglese dell'Ottocento sulle rive dello Jonio: George Gissing," *Bollettino del comune di Taranto*, XXXII (1963), no. 96, pp. 14-31.

Gabriele Armandi, "Gissing in Calabria," *Osservatore Romano*, 5 July 1978, p. 7.

Ernesta and Albert Spencer Mills, "Biografie di viaggiatori inglesi in Calabria (3): George Gissing (1857-1903)," *Calabria Sconosciuta*, April-June 1980, pp. 24-27.

Francesco Badolato, "George Gissing in Calabria," *Calabria*, October 1985, p. 74.

Rosario Manes, "Un inglese a Paola," *Calabria Sconosciuta*, April-June 1990, pp. 69-70.

Mauro F. Minervino, *La Vita desiderata: George R. Gissing, un vittoriano al sud* (Cosenza, 1993).

Raffaele La Capria, "Italiani, magnifici selvaggi," *Corriere della sera*, 8 April 1994, p. 31.

Francesco Badolato, "Catanzaro in G. Gissing, F. Lenormant e N. Douglas," *Calabria Sconosciuta*, April-June 1994, pp. 37-39. Similar articles by the same author appeared on Reggio in July-September 1994, pp. 65-68, on Cosenza in January-March 1995, pp. 81-83 and on Squillace in January-March 1996, pp. 53-56.

Annarita del Nobile, "Viaggio e scritturra: Il tragetto ideologico di George Gissing in Italia," *Tracce*, June-September 1994, pp. 56-59. Translated in the *Gissing Journal*, January 1997, pp. 19-22.

Virgilio Squillace, "Ecco l'albergo di Gissing, Douglas, Lenormant," *Gazzetta del Sud*, 1 April 1997 and "Dal 'Concordia' all'"Italia'," 6 April 1997.

Anon., "La curiosità: Cosí l'albergatore Paparazzo diventò fotoreporter," *Corriere della sera*, 2 September 1997, p. 7.

Francesco Badolato, "Viaggiatori dell'Ottocento: Gissing e Sculco," *Il Crotonese*, 11-14 December 1998, p. 12.

Anon., "Alla scoperta di Gissing," *Il Domani della Calabria*, 17 October 1999, p. 14 ; and in the same newspaper, Paola Cosentino, "Nel ricordo del 'nostro' Gissing," 24 October 1999, p. 14.

George Gissing, *La terra del sole: Lettere dall'Italia e dalla Grecia (1888-1898)*, ed. Francesco Badolato (Soveria Mannelli, 1999).

Mauro Francesco Minervino, "Mr. Paparazzo, I presume," *Diario della settimana*, 29 March-4 April 2000, pp. 20-31.

Aurelio Fulciniti, *Catanzaro Ieri e Oggi* (Catanzaro, 2001). Contains a chapter on Gissing.

Carla Capece Minutolo, *Catanzaro Città di Storia e di Cultura* (Catanzaro, 2001).

Giovanni Guarascio, "Un convegno del Rotary Club sul soggiorno crotonese di François Lenormant, George Gissing e Norman Douglas," *Gazzetta del Sud*, 25 June 2002, p. 27.

Mauro Francesco Minervino (ed.), *George Gissing a Catanzaro: Atti del Convegno Internazionale di Studi Catanzaro 23 ottobre 1999* (Catanzaro, 2002).

V Books about Calabria: Historical, Literary and Topographical Aspects

The guide books for tourists available in Gissing's lifetime were those that he himself mentions and carried in his luggage: *Murray's Handbook for Travellers in Southern Italy and Sicily*, Part I, and Karl Baedeker's *Southern Italy and Sicily: Handbook for Travellers*. Augustus J. C. Hare's well-documented volume, *Cities of Southern Italy and Sicily*, could also prove a serviceable companion, quoting as he does from historians and travellers, notably Gibbon, Craufurd Tait Ramage and Lenormant. A far more modern guide book in Italian and French is *Incontro con la Calabria/ Découvrir la Calabre* by Domenico Laruffa (Reggio Calabria, 1984), while a suggestive, commented listing of foreign travellers who wrote books on Calabria will be found in *Gli scrittori stranieri e la Calabria* (Cosenza, n.d.). A valuable illustrated French guide book is that by Georges and Huguette Vallet, *Naples et l'Italie du Sud* (Paris, 1966).

Most useful to Gissing before, during and after his journey was the masterly study of Magna Græcia by François Lenormant, *La Grande-Grèce: Paysages et Histoire* (3 vols., 1881-84), which partakes of archaeology, history and topography. No other modern work influenced him more deeply.

Among the travellers whose experiences are worth comparing with Gissing's are Germans who explored Calabria in the late eighteenth century, for instance Johann Hermann von Riedesel (*Reise durch Sizilien und Grossgriechenland*, 1771), Johann Heinrich Bartels (*Briefe über Kalabrien und Sizilien*, 1787) and Friedrich Leopold Stolberg (*Reise in Italien*, 1794). Of all the French, the best-known commentator was perhaps Paul Bourget, whose *Sensations d'Italie* (1891) Gissing had read, while among English and American writers who followed more or less consciously in his footsteps were Norman Douglas, author of *Siren Land* (1911) and more importantly *Old Calabria* (1915), Edward Hutton with his erudite *Naples and Southern Italy* (1915), and Henry James

Forman who, like Douglas and Hutton, was anxious to see the albergo where Gissing struggled for days with fever, and who grew eloquent about it in *Grecian Italy* (1927). Maria Brandon-Albini, in her French volume *Calabre* (1957), offers a transition to more recent travellers who were bent on identifying topographical details noted by Gissing, for instance Paul Theroux in his *Pillars of Hercules* (1995) or John Keahey, whose express aim in *A Sweet and Glorious Land: Revisiting the Ionian Sea* (2000) was to retrace Gissing's footsteps. In a sense the ancestor of all these travelogues is *The Nooks and Byways of Italy* by Craufurd Tait Ramage, published in 1868, and currently available under the title *Ramage in South Italy*, abridged and edited by Edith Clay (Chicago, 1987).

A large number of profusely illustrated monographs on Calabria and on the towns visited by Gissing have been published in Italy, mainly by Rubbettino Editore, of Soveria Mannelli, for instance :

Beppe Mazzocca and Antonio Panzarella (eds.), *Cara Catanzaro*, 1987. In their series, *Le Città della Calabria: Storia, Cultura, Economia*, edited by Fulvio Mazza, they have devoted very substantial volumes to Catanzaro (1994), Cosenza (1991), Crotone (1992) and Reggio (1993).

Also of interest are :

Luigi Parpagliolo, *Italia* (negli scrittori italiani e stranieri), Volume VII Calabria (Polistena, R.C.: Tipolitografia Varamo, 1993).

Agazio Trombetta, *Saluti da Reggio Calabria: Radici e immagini* (Reggio Calabria: Corpododici Edizioni, 1993).

Sergio Dragone, *Catanzaro: I luoghi, le persone, la storia* (Catanzaro: Cinesud due Editore, 4 volumes, 1995).

Renato Sandrini, *La Calabria* (Catanzaro: Mario Giuditta Editore, 1996).

Mimmo Jodice, *Old Calabria: I luoghi del Grand Tour* (Milan: Federico Motta, 2000).